HOW TO
GOLD LEAF
ANTIQUES

and other art objects

HOW TO
GOLD LEAF
ANTIQUES

and other art objects

Techniques of an ancient art explained step by step
in how-to-do-it text and pictures

DONALD L. CHAMBERS

CROWN PUBLISHERS, INC., NEW YORK

Inquiries should be addressed to Crown Publishers, Inc.,
419 Park Avenue South, New York, N.Y. 10016.

Library of Congress Catalog Card Number: 72-96672
ISBN: 0-517-503557

Printed in the United States of America
Published simultaneously in Canada by
General Publishing Company Limited

Designed by Ruth Smerechniak

Acknowledgments

My sincere thanks to Cliff Sewell, whose newspaper articles persuaded me that this book was needed; to Dr. Lewis M. Davis for his skill and patience in taking the photographs, and Virginia Davis for her encouragement; to collectors James A. Williams, Mrs. J. Fred Schwalb, Arthur Smith, and Julian H. Head for permission to show their antiques in the process of restoration; and to the many amateur artists and craftsmen whose questions prompted this publication of the answers.

D.L.C.

Contents

Preface

Gold leafing, or *gilding* as it is called, is an art as old as recorded history. For thousands of years it has been practiced by skilled craftsmen to beautify many kinds of things we live with or see around us.

There is no doubt that the use of gold leaf played an important part in the artistic development of early civilizations. The temples, tombs, and palaces of ancient cultures—notably the Chinese, Japanese, and Egyptian—were profusely adorned with gilded murals and gold-covered furnishings. Greek and Roman sculptors embellished their carvings with gold, and stonemasons gilded the incised lettering of inscriptions on the white Carrara marble of buildings. Art of the Middle Ages gleamed with gold leaf, and recluse monks in European monasteries diligently illuminated the vellum pages of their holy books with burnished gold.

During the past few hundred years gold-leafed furnishings have come to be valued, increasingly, as a kind of status symbol. In the nineteenth century, in France and England, they were thought to be essential to the decor of an important person's residence. In America, when the White House was rebuilt after it had been burned by the British in 1814, much of the new furniture was of "gilt-wood" (gold-leafed wood) ordered from France. It naturally followed that both wealthy and middle-class Americans were influenced to copy the style. The possession of fine, gold-leafed furnishings became a mark of distinction; to a considerable degree it still is.

What is this magic, yellow material called gold leaf? Contrary to common belief, it is not a liquid; it is not applied with a brush, like paint. As its name implies it is a small sheet or leaf of pure gold, beaten so thin that a faint puff of air sends it fluttering across the room. When properly affixed to an object, this leaf is amazingly durable. It can be burnished to the rich brilliance of polished jewelry and, if not abused, will retain its luster indefinitely.

Gold leaf can be used to decorate almost anything, but certain objects lend themselves naturally to surfacing with this lustrous metal. Today the most familiar of these objects are frames for pictures or mirrors, wood carvings, figurines, clocks, lamps, bookends, architectural moldings, and numerous articles of furniture. The most profitable and aesthetically rewarding use for gold leaf is in the restoration of antiques that originally were gilded, but which have been abused or allowed to fall into disrepair.

For centuries the so-called secrets of applying and burnishing gold leaf were handed down from father to son, or taught by artisans to their apprentices. There always has been a wide demand for the products of this craft, and in our grandparents' time there apparently was no shortage of expert gilders, if we can judge by the large numbers of gold-leafed objects we have inherited. These antiques are rapidly disappearing. Most of them are, today, in sad need of restoration.

Unfortunately the gilding skills have become a neglected and, indeed, *almost* a lost art. Relatively few proficient gilders are to be found, and their services are absorbed by art galleries and manufacturers of expensive new frames and furniture. Even in large metropolitan cities few art dealers or picture framers can provide goldleafing services for their customers.

Consequently, today most private owners have no alternative but must have their prized antiques or cherished heirlooms "restored" with gold-colored paint or wax or other imitation materials. The resultant finish is obviously counterfeit and the gilt soon tarnishes. Even if real gold is used, few restorers know how to burnish it to the rich luster that characterized the original work.

In the face of scarcity, the demand for gold-leafing services is steadily increasing. Hence, these services could become a source of profit to framers, art dealers, restorers, and artists who will make them available to the public. And gold leafing can be a fascinating *and financially profitable* avocation or hobby for amateurs. It is not nearly as difficult as it may seem at first try. With patience and practice almost anyone can learn to apply and burnish gold leaf. This book tells how.

1

Repairing Damage

THE INSTRUCTIONS THAT FOLLOW CAN GUIDE YOU IN GOLD LEAFING ALMOST ANY-thing, new or old. Probably the most plentiful of once-gilded objects are antique frames. They are seen everywhere in all shapes and sizes, and they seem to cry out for restoration. Therefore—in describing the basic gilding procedures that apply to *all* objects—we shall discuss, as a typical example, the step-by-step restoration of an old frame.

GILDING vs. GOLD LEAFING

There is a natural confusion about the usage of the terms *gilding* and *gold leafing*. Gilding is the older. It means to cover with *any kind* of gold-, silver-, or bronzelike material—including pure gold. When you coat an antique with metallic, gold-colored paint, you are *gilding* it, even though the paint does not contain an atom of real gold. If you use genuine gold leaf, you are gilding it. Or, if you apply a silver-colored paint made of powdered aluminum, you still are gilding it.

The term *gold leafing*, however, is specific. It means only one thing—to cover with actual leaves of real gold. You may *gild* with imitation gold leaf, but you cannot *gold leaf* with it.

This usage of the terms has prevailed for a long, long time, and we shall stick with it. In this book the term *gilding* is applied to the use of any gold-, silver-, or bronzelike material, including real gold.

11

Gilded antiques suffer damage over the years from many causes. Generations of owners may have rubbed the lustrous surfaces bare with coarse abrasive cleansers or strong detergents. Hanging objects fall from walls and are cracked or broken. Careless handling, storage, dirt, and dampness take their toll. Whatever the causes may have been, your first step in gold leafing any object is to repair the damage and put the piece in good structural condition. This is especially true of an old frame. It would be a waste of time, effort, and materials to gild a frame that is loose at the mitered corners, or on which the appliqued ornaments are not securely fastened.

This antique frame is broken and chipped. Some small parts are missing, and the original gold leaf is almost gone. We shall repair and releaf it on the following pages.

Enlargement shows kind of damage commonly found in old frames.

Inspect the frame carefully. Make all repairs that seem necessary, with special attention to the following:

Tightening Loose Joints

If a corner joint has separated or is not entirely tight, force it apart sufficiently to clean the opened surfaces with a strip of coarse sandpaper; then reglue, and drive the original nails back into place. "5 Minute" Epoxy, a glue available in tubes at hardware and paint stores, is recommended for a quick, strong bond. This glue is a convenient time-saver and is very useful for joints that cannot be clamped. You hold the joint together with your fingers, and the glue sets in five minutes.

If necessary, replace the original corner nails with new ones that are slightly larger. If you do the nailing *immediately* after applying the glue, neither clamps nor fingers will be needed to hold the joint until the glue sets.

A gluing precaution: the joints of an old frame may be so loose that the four sides will twist until they are neither square nor flat. Don't glue them together this way. When you apply the glue, have the frame lying on a flat, level surface; use a T square to square up the sides.

Before gluing, inner liners are removed and all parts of the frame are wiped clean.

"5 Minute" Epoxy glue is available in tubes at hardware and paint stores. There is also a slow-setting type that allows more working time.

Mix equal parts of resin and hardener. Mixing must be thorough, and the glue must be applied quickly before it sets.

Discardable sticks or toothpicks are better than brushes for mixing small quantities. If you get the glue on your fingers, wipe it off with denatured alcohol before it hardens.

Fitting Inner Liners

Most antique frames have one or more inner liners. These are separate sections that fit into each other and give the frame depth. Treat each liner as though it were a separate frame. After tightening and gluing the corners, see that the liners fit into each other and into the outer frame with very little play. If the spaces between them are too wide, take up the slack by gluing thin strips of wood where needed along the inner sides.

Keep the liners and the outer frame separate. *They must be gilded separately*, then nailed back in place after all gilding has been completed.

Replacing Missing Ornaments

The ornaments on a frame are the raised decorations that have been applied to the frame's wooden foundation molding. Sometimes they are carved wood, but usually they are made of a plaster composition. They become loose or broken, and often are missing.

If ornaments are loose, remove and clean them, then glue them back firmly in place. Ornaments that are starting to crack but are not very loose may be secured by pushing glue gently into the cracks with a thin knife or a toothpick. Use epoxy glue for large, heavy ornaments, and any standard "milk" glue, such as Elmer's, for the cracks.

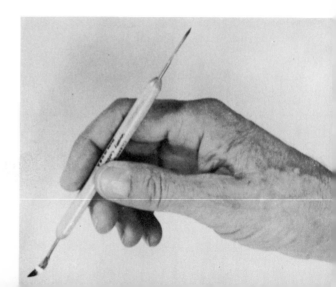

A ceramics clean-up tool is useful for many gilding purposes.

If small pieces are broken off ornaments, replace them with plastic wood or a hard-setting modeling compound. Shape them in place with your fingers, a small knife, or a stick. A handy little device for shaping small replacements is a ceramics clean-up tool, available at any ceramics-supplies store.

If a large section of ornament is missing, you may need to replace it by making a mold and casting. This will not be too difficult if an identical ornament is present on another part of the frame; it often is. You can make a mold of the existing ornament, then use the mold to cast a duplicate ornament which you can glue in place. (See *How to Make a Mold and Casting*, p.00.)

If large areas of ornamentation are missing and you cannot replace them with castings, you may need to have the work done by a professional artist or a talented amateur—unless, of course, you are personally able to sculpture the missing parts in plaster or wood. This may be a time to decide whether or not the frame is sufficiently valuable to justify the expense of professional assistance.

Perhaps all the ornaments are intact except for parts (or all) of a thinly embossed border strip. These borders have a habit of falling off. Because of their thinness they are hard to replace with castings. There is an easy solution to the problem: a number of American manufacturers supply reproductions of hand-carved borders which can be purchased by the linear foot. They are inexpensive and easy to glue in place. (See *Ready-made Ornaments*, p. 80.)

Cleaning Carved Ornaments

Often, on old frames, the hollows of carved ornaments and decorative borders have become filled in by repeated applications of gold paint or other coatings. If your frame has received such treatment, you can unclog the hollows with paint remover. A semipaste type is recommended because it does not readily run off. Apply it freely; allow it to stand about fifteen minutes; rub gently with a small, stiff bristle brush (a stencil brush is good); then wipe with a cloth and flush with denatured alcohol. Alcohol neutralizes the caustic action of paint remover. Repeat this procedure if necessary, but *do not leave paint remover on plaster parts of the frame long enough to soften them.*

Smoothing the Frame

At this point your frame is sound and clean. Examine it for surface imperfections. Use plastic wood to fill in cracks, nail holes, deep scars, and spots where the original wood or plaster has been chipped or gouged away. Sandpaper the filled-in places until they are flush with the surface. Then sandpaper the entire frame—*with the exception of carved or embossed parts*—until the surfaces are quite smooth. Use 3/0 or 4/0 finishing paper on rough places; smooth the flat surfaces with 6/0 or 7/0 finishing paper.

When sanding flat surfaces you may wrap the finishing paper around a

To make a sanding block, saw a flat piece of wood to the desired size. As a rule, power sanders should not be used on antiques.

You can make fine or coarse cylindrical sanders, of any diameter, by wrapping abrasive paper around pieces of doweling.

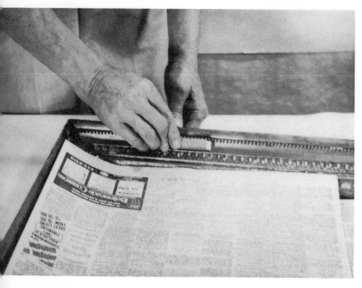

The doweling lessens wear and tear on the fingers and helps to smooth channels more evenly, with less danger of sanding away outer edges.

small, flat block of wood to insure an even cutting pressure. If the frame has concave flutings or channels, they may be smoothed more evenly if you wrap the finishing paper around a piece of doweling that is slightly smaller in diameter than the width of the channel. All sizes of doweling are sold by hardware stores.

Usually it is not practical to try to smooth the small carved or raised ornaments or the intricate relief work found in many frames. You may, however, smooth their raised surfaces by rubbing them gently with 2/0 or 3/0 steel wool. Be careful when using finishing paper or steel wool not to wear down the raised surfaces and thus efface the design.

In the final smoothing, be sure to erase all traces of old gold leaf. If you don't, the coats of gesso you will apply next may later crack loose from the surface.

GRIT SIZES OF ABRASIVE PAPERS

Abrasive papers are graded from coarse to fine according to the size of their sharp-edged grains of "sand." The grains on coarse papers are large and cut quickly and deeply, leaving scratches. On fine papers the grains are small and cut slowly. These are called *finishing* papers because they are used for final smoothing; the scratches they leave may be almost imperceptible.

Different hard minerals are ground to make the cutting grains. For gilding purposes, most fine smoothing is done with either garnet or aluminum oxide papers; silicon carbide papers are used for the very finest smoothing.

The coarseness or fineness of abrasive papers is printed on their uncoated sides in terms of (1) the approximate number of grains in a linear inch, as 180; or (2) a relative numerical grading, as 5/0. Thus, if the paper is marked 180, it is also 5/0, and vice versa.

In this book, the fineness of finishing papers is stated as 4/0, 6/0, 9/0, and so on; the higher the number, the finer the grit. Because some brands of papers are not marked both ways, we give the following table:

/0 = 80	6/0 = 220
2/0 = 100	7/0 = 240
3/0 = 120	8/0 = 280
4/0 = 150	9/0 = 320
5/0 = 180	10/0 = 400

2

Preparing the Surface for Gilding

THE FRAME IS NOW READY TO RECEIVE A FOUNDATION COATING OVER WHICH YOU will apply an adhesive, called *size*, and lay the gold leaf. The purpose of this coating is to provide a perfectly smooth surface, without which the finished work would not be satisfactory. The coating also serves as a cushion on the areas you later will polish by rubbing with an agate burnisher.

Applying a Gesso Foundation

Old-time gilders found that a preparation of finely powdered chalk, or whiting, with glue added made an excellent foundation coating. They called it *gesso*, and its modern counterparts are sold today by that name. In smoothing your frame, if it is an old one, you no doubt have exposed the gesso foundation put on by the original gilder.

Until recent years gilders used their own formulas and mixed their own gesso. Some still do, but it is no longer necessary. Many forms of prepared gesso are now being sold, used chiefly as grounds (foundation coatings) for artists' canvases and panels. Some of these preparations are not suitable for gilding purposes, but a few are. The dry form, which must be mixed with cold water, is the best. One brand recommended as a gilding foundation is Gesso Ground Dry Mixture, manufactured by Permanent Pigments, Inc. (see *Gilding Supplies*, p. 108).

Mixing Gesso

Mix the dry gesso with distilled water, following directions on the container label. Some manufacturers state proportions by *weight*, others by

Materials and tools used in mixing gesso: dry gesso mixture, distilled
water, measuring cup, spoon, widemouthed jar.

volume. If you are using the Permanent Pigments product, mix by volume
as follows:

1. Use an 8-ounce measuring cup. Into a widemouthed jar pour 1 cupful
of cold distilled water. Add 2 cupfuls of dry gesso. Stir. Cover the jar and
allow the mixture to stand overnight.

2. Next day, place the jar of gesso in a saucepan of hot water. Stir occasionally until the mixture is warm and quite smooth. Reheat the water if it
becomes cool. The gesso should now be about the consistency of heavy
cream and ready to apply. It will keep for months if the jar is tightly covered.

First, pour the water into the jar . . .   Add the dry gesso . . .

Stir, and let the mixture
stand overnight.

Applying Gesso

Gesso should be kept quite warm but not hot while it is being applied. If it has cooled, place the jar again in hot water and stir until the mixture liquefies. Then follow these directions:

1. Pour some gesso into a cup and place the cup in a pan of very warm water. A heavy custard cup will hold the heat and "stay put" on the bottom of the pan better than a thin teacup. Keep a teaspoon in the cup and stir every few minutes while applying. Reheat the water as often as necessary. (Reheating interruptions can be eliminated by using a small, inexpensive heating unit such as those used by office workers to heat their cups of instant coffee.)

2. Use a flat, soft brush. An ox-hair brush is good; a sable brush is better but more expensive. Select brush widths suited to the areas to be covered. You may need a ¾-inch width for wide panels, and a ¼-inch for embossed moldings and the hollows of carved ornaments.

3. Brush the gesso on thinly. Do not allow it to puddle and clog small hollows. If the mixture becomes too thick, thin it with a little water.

4. Apply three or more coats until the frame is well covered. Allow each coat to dry thoroughly—1 to 2 hours—before applying the next coat. Then smooth the surface with 6/0 or 7/0 finishing paper until brush marks have disappeared. Be very gentle when rubbing the high surfaces of ornaments and embossed borders.

5. Now apply two more, and final, coats. These should be flowed on smoothly *to cover only the flat or high surfaces you have just smoothed with finishing paper*. Wait at least 3 hours after the last coat. Then complete the gessoing with a final smoothing. Use 8/0 finishing paper on the flat areas, and *4/0 steel wool only* on the small carved or embossed areas.

COLORED GESSO

Dry gesso may be colored to any desired shade by adding *dry colors* after the gesso has been mixed with water. If you intend to "antique" mat-leafed surfaces by rubbing through the leaf (as explained on page 64) you should color the last two or three coats of gesso applied to these surfaces. A dark, reddish brown color is the most effective. Use a coloring product recommended on the gesso container. If this is your first gilding experience, however, we suggest that you forgo the rubbed antiquing.

After warming the gesso, pour some into a cup. Place the cup in a pan of hot water, ready for application.

Small immersion heaters are sold in many stores. On-off switches must be purchased separately.

A narrow, sable brush is best for covering carved surfaces with gesso. Five or six coats usually are needed. The last two coats should be applied only to the tops of the carving.

Deciding What Parts to Burnish

Your treatment of the frame at this point must depend on *the kind of finish you wish to achieve.* Many kinds of finishes can be produced with gold leaf, but we need consider here only the two kinds most commonly desired:

1. *Mat finish.* A surface is said to be *mat* when it is dull, or without brilliance. The word (often spelled matte) is used in reference to art techniques and artists' materials that produce a dull rather than a shiny surface. A mat gold-leafed surface has a rich, dull luster.

2. *Burnish finish.* To "burnish" is to cause to shine, especially by rubbing. The word is applied most often to the polishing of metals. Gold leaf is burnished by rubbing it with an agate burnisher, giving the surface a mirrorlike brilliance.

Some gilded objects have an entirely mat finish; others are entirely burnished; most, however, have both mat and burnished parts. The contrast of dullness and brilliance contributes greatly to an object's beauty. Usually the raised surfaces of a frame, especially those on the ornaments, and the convex columns and concave channels of the molding are burnished. Large, flat areas and deeply recessed parts of ornaments are not burnished.

The frame we are restoring will have both mat and burnished parts: the flat, innermost liner will be mat leafed. The middle liner and the outer frame will be burnished—and the stippled border between them will be mat leafed.

Treating Parts to Be Mat Leafed

The frame now has a smooth, gesso surface. The parts that are to be mat leafed must be sealed with shellac. Sealing is necessary because the gesso foundation is porous; if not sealed, the adhesive size you later will apply to it may be partially absorbed.

Either clear or orange shellac may be used. Orange is preferred because its color will plainly mark the parts that are not to be burnished. *Do not put shellac on parts that are to be burnished.* If you accidentally do so, rub it off after it dries with 8/0 finishing paper.

Thin the shellac by adding denatured alcohol or a commercial shellac thinner such as Solux, in the proportion of 2 parts shellac to 1 part alcohol. Apply two coats with a flat sable brush, allowing 2 hours drying time between coats. Smooth the shellacked surfaces by rubbing them very lightly with 4/0 steel wool until brush marks have disappeared.

Treating Parts to Be Burnished

Parts of the frame that are to be burnished must be coated with *burnish size.* This is applied over the gesso foundation, but only to the parts that have not been sealed with shellac. *Before proceeding, read the description of Gold Sizes on page 24.*

Preparing Burnish Size

The first time you mix burnish size, it will seem complicated; the second time, you'll understand it; the third time, it will be easy. Follow these steps:

1. Into a large glass pour ½ pint (1 cup) of cold, distilled water; add ½ ounce of granular rabbit skin glue, and stir. Cover the glass and allow the mixture to stand overnight. Accurate measurement will be easy if you use a graduated measuring cup for the water, and weigh the glue on a small postal letter scale, available for a few dollars at stationery stores.

Materials and tools used in mixing rabbit skin glue solution: measuring cup, granulated glue, postal scale, spoon, distilled water, glass.

Accurate measurement is important. Use a graduated measuring cup for the distilled water. Pour the water into a glass . . .

Weigh the rabbit skin glue on a small postal scale . . .

Pour the glue into the water and stir. Cover the glass and let the mixture stand overnight.

GOLD SIZES

In gilding techniques the term *size* means any material used to seal the pores of a surface or serve as an adhesive, or both. Two kinds of sizes are used in laying gold leaf on antiques and art objects. They are: (1) *oil-type gold size* for surfaces to be mat leafed; and (2) *burnish size* for surfaces to be burnished.

Oil-type Gold Size

Oil-type gold size is a varnishlike liquid that is applied with a brush. There are two kinds—quick drying and slow drying. Quick-drying size usually becomes tacky enough to receive the leaf 1 to 2 hours after it has been applied; the time depends on atmospheric conditions: warm, dry weather hastens the action.

Slow-drying size may take 12 hours or more to become tacky enough for gilding. It retains its tackiness for many hours, thus permitting careful and leisurely laying of the leaf. If possible, a surface coated with slow-drying size should be protected from dust before the leaf is laid.

Some gilders believe that leaf laid over quick-drying size is not as brilliant as that laid over slow-drying size; others believe there is little difference, if any. Quick-drying size picks up less dust from the air, and is more practical for small jobs that can be completed in a short time.

Burnish Size

Burnish size is a finely ground clay called *bole*. It is sold as a water-base paste about the consistency of lard but much heavier. It comes in a number of colors—red, yellow, blue, and gray—for various gilding purposes. Red is preferred for most uses because it imparts a deep, rich tone to the applied leaf which, because of its thinness, is slightly transparent. Jars of this clay are usually labeled "gold size," but the clay is not a *size* until a rabbit skin glue solution is added.

Gold sizes and rabbit skin glue are sold or can be obtained by art-supplies stores. A leading manufacturer of the sizes is Hastings & Co., Philadelphia. (See *Gilding Supplies*, p. 108.)

2. After allowing the glue to soak, place the glass in a pan of hot (not steaming) water and stir until the glue granules have completely dissolved. Keep the solution quite warm but not hot; rabbit skin glue loses its adhesive strength if overheated.

3. Open a jar of red burnish size and stir the clay with a teaspoon until it is smooth and creamy. Into a china or earthenware cup (do not use a metal container) place 1 tablespoon of size and 3 tablespoons of warm glue solution. Use a marked measuring spoon for accuracy. Stir until thoroughly mixed. It is best to add the glue solution a spoonful at a time while stirring.

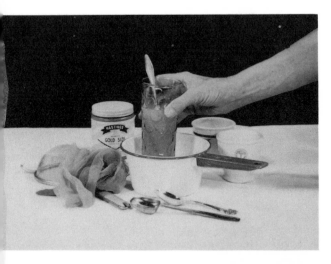

The first step in mixing burnish size is to warm the glue solution in a pan of hot water.

Stir the red clay until it is creamy smooth. If the clay has become too thick, add a little distilled water.

Accurate measuring spoons are sold in sets by many kinds of stores.

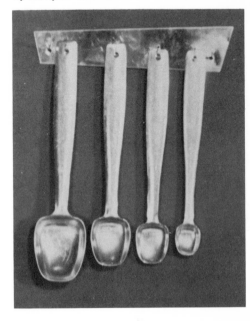

Burnish size adheres like mud. Use a finger to push it from the measuring spoon into the cup.

4. Strain the mixture immediately into another cup through several layers of a fine-mesh nylon stocking. Straining can be made easy and less messy by pulling a nylon stocking *half* inside out and inserting a 4-inch-diameter wire-mesh strainer into the opening. This will put two layers of nylon on top of the strainer and two layers on the bottom. With a spoon, depress the top layers of nylon into the hollow of the strainer, then pour the warm mixture through this device.

The burnish size is now ready for application, but you need not hurry. It will not hurt the size if it stands an hour or two before being used.

Before applying the burnish size, brush all particles of sanded gesso from the corners and ornaments. Wipe the frame with a clean, soft cloth. If you have a reversible vacuum cleaner, it can be used to blow sanding dust from recesses and hollows.

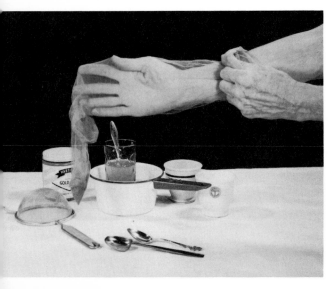

There's a trick to getting the stocking on the strainer. First, pull the stocking half inside out over your wrist . . .

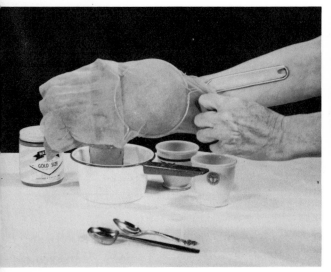

. . . slide the strainer inside, and place it over an empty cup.

Pour the mixed size through the strainer into the cup. It is now ready to apply.

Applying Burnish Size

Work in a warm, dust-free room. Keep the size quite warm but not hot, by placing the cup in a pan of very warm water. The method is the same as you used in applying gesso except that you must be more careful not to let the size become hot. If it does, it may "pinhole" and not adhere evenly to the surface. Keep a teaspoon in the cup and stir the mixture every few minutes while applying.

Brush the size freely, *only onto the surfaces to be burnished.* Use a flat sable brush. The width of the brush should be determined by the width of the parts to be covered; ⅝ inch is a practical, general-use width, but you may need both a narrower and a wider brush for different parts of the frame.

When dipping the brush, do not wipe it on the edge of the cup. Such wiping produces a granular accumulation of drying clay within the cup, and it may carry air bubbles into the mixture.

First, impregnate the dry brush by dipping it in the size almost to the ferrule; then, in two strokes, draw both flat sides of the brush lightly over a piece of paper, and lay the almost-dry brush down for a minute. From then on, carry the brush directly from size to surface, with no wiping. You can control the amount of size needed for each stroke by the depth you dip the brush into the cup.

Flow the size on in one direction, with as little stroking as possible. Five or six coats usually are required, with a smoothing in between. The size dries quickly, so you need not wait long between coats. A safe rule is to wait ½ hour after all damp spots from the preceding coat have disappeared.

After the third coat, allow about 1 hour's drying time and smooth the surface lightly with 8/0 finishing paper. Then brush and wipe the frame clean of sanding dust and apply the last two or three coats.

Important: Mix fresh glue solution and burnish size for each day's work. If mixed burnish size is kept over and used the next day, its glue content may lose its strength.

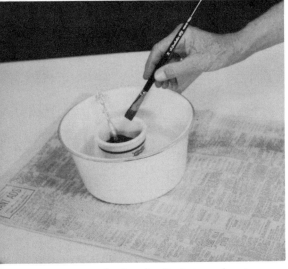

To impregnate the brush, dip it into the size . . .

. . . then draw each side of the brush lightly over a piece of paper.

Smoothing Burnish Size

The brilliance of your finished work will depend largely on the smoothness you now give the burnish-sized surface. Smooth it again with finishing paper. This time, however, observe these precautions against rubbing off too much size:

1. Use 10/0 instead of 8/0 paper. If this is not available, use 500-grit or 600-grit silicon carbide paper.

2. Rub with very gentle pressure. Do not attempt to smooth recesses or *small* carved surfaces.

Either 10/0 finishing paper or 500-grit silicon carbide paper may be used to smooth the sized surface. Paper shown here is silicon carbide.

3. If you accidentally rub through the red size in a few places, paint these spots with fresh burnish size. Gold leaf will not adhere to places that are not covered with an adhesive.

If you wish to produce a very high brilliance, polish the burnish-sized surface further by rubbing it with an agate burnisher (see *Burnishing Gold Leaf*, p. 49). *Caution:* A burnisher used to polish burnish size should be kept separate for that purpose only; it should not be used to burnish gold leaf.

*   *   *   *   *   *

At this point the preparatory work has been accomplished. The frame is ready to receive the gold leaf. Before proceeding, study the following information on Handling Gold Leaf. *Then continue by* Applying Gold Leaf (p. 34).

3

Handling Gold Leaf

THIS BRIEF EXPLANATION OF THE NATURE OF GOLD LEAF WILL HELP YOU UNDER-stand some problems you will encounter when first handling it. "Handling" may not be the right word, because the leaf is so thin it disintegrates and seems to disappear when touched with a finger. Snow White's seven dwarfs would have been poor gilders; the air currents from their whistling would have sent the gold leaf flying. The leaf is readily manipulated, however, with simple, inexpensive tools designed for the purpose. Don't be discouraged if you lose some gold while learning to use these tools.

Pure gold is too soft for most commercial uses: it must be hardened by adding other metal to make an alloy. The fineness, or purity, of gold is measured in terms of "karats." In this usage, a *karat* is *one twenty-fourth*. Thus, pure gold is 24 karats, or 24/24 pure. Most gold leaf is 23 karats, or 23/24 pure. Only 1 part in 24 is other metal. By comparison, the gold in a "solid gold" piece of jewelry usually is 14 karats, or only 14/24 pure. So the gold leaf you will use is about as pure as gold can be for commercial or artistic purposes.

Gold leaf is costly—partly because of the metal's value, but mostly because expensive processing and highly trained craftsmen are required in its manufacture. However, a little gold leaf goes a long way in restoring an average-size frame or other art object.

How Gold Leaf Is Packaged

Gold leaf is packaged in what are called *books*, each containing 25 leaves of gold. The leaves are 3⅜ inches square and are separated in the book by thin paper tissues. Retail dealers usually buy the leaf from manufacturers in *packs*, each pack containing 20 books.

The books of leaf are prepared in two forms: (1) *loose packed*, with the leaves of gold lying loose between the separating tissues, and (2) *patent—* also called *transfer leaf*—in which each leaf of gold adheres lightly to a paper tissue on which it may be lifted from the book and applied to the object by hand. (Other sizes of leaf and forms of packaging are available for various specialized purposes.)

Loose-packed leaf can be used for all gilding purposes *if applied indoors*. It is difficult to apply outdoors because even a slight breeze would blow the leaves out of control. *Only the loose-packed leaf can be used satisfactorily on surfaces that are to be burnished.*

Patent leaf is designed especially for outside work where air currents are prevalent. However, it may be used very effectively on flat areas of an object and on many rounded, concave, and convex parts *provided they are not to be burnished*. Patent leaf must be laid over oil-type size, as explained later.

Gold leaf is sold in several shades. For most gilding, the preferred color is natural, *deep gold*. This color, when loose packed, is labeled "XX Deep 23-Karat," and the package may carry the words "For Glass," because the loose, deep leaf is used for lettering signs on glass windows and doors. Patent leaf is the same deep gold color. It is labeled "XX Deep Patent" and usually is 23 karat. Other colors are pale gold, lemon gold, and green gold. These are alloys and have a lower gold content; they must be given protective coatings to prevent them from tarnishing.

Preparing Gold Leaf for Application

Loose-packed leaf must be removed from the book and laid on the object without being touched by fingers. Full-size leaves are sometimes applied in gilding large objects. Usually, however, the leaf must be cut or torn into smaller pieces that can be laid with minimal waste.

Old records indicate that gilders always have been plagued by the problem of transferring a perverse piece of gold leaf from one place to another. The old-timers tried many methods and came up with one that remains in wide use today. The technique has its points, but it requires long practice to perfect. We do not recommend it for the gilding of antiques and art objects. However, because it has been so generally used, we shall describe it briefly for you to try if you like:

An Old Method

1. Make or buy a *gilder's cushion* on which to cut the leaf. The cushion is made of a piece of wood about ½ inch thick, 6 inches wide, and 9 inches long. Put a ¼-inch-thick raw-cotton padding on the top, and over this tack a smooth piece of leather, unfinished side up. Then tack a cardboard "windshield" about 3 inches high around the back, extending 4 inches forward along each side.

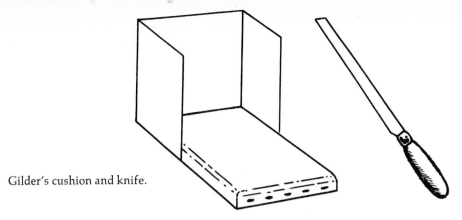

Gilder's cushion and knife.

2. Obtain a *gilder's knife*. It has a long, straight blade, free of nicks and rather dull. It is used to cut the leaf without tearing the edges. A suitably shaped kitchen carving knife may be dulled and used for this purpose.

3. Open a book of loose-packed leaf and blow, with very gentle puffs, several leaves of gold into the back of the cushion, against the cardboard shield.

4. Slide the knife under one of the leaves, lift the leaf, and lay it as flatly as possible on the front part of the cushion. Puff gently on the leaf to flatten out wrinkles.

5. Cut the leaf to desired sizes by resting the knife edge across the entire leaf, pushing it away from you about ⅛ inch, and then drawing it toward you until it has entirely cleared the leaf and the cushion. No pressure should be used, except the weight of the knife.

6. After cutting, separate the pieces of leaf from each other by sliding them apart, one at a time, on a flat side of the knife.

7. Have at hand a *gilder's tip*. Use it in applying the leaf to the object, as described under *Laying Leaf on Burnish Size* (p. 35).

An Easier Method

If you use this method, disregard the preceding instructions for *An Old Method*. With very little practice the following steps will become almost automatic:

1. Cover your worktable with fresh, clean paper; unwrinkled newspaper will do.

2. With a pair of sharp scissors, cut off the binding edge of a book of loose-packed leaf. Hold the book in the fingers of your left hand and slide the cut edge between the thumb and index finger of your right hand, bending the

The binding edge of the book is cut off with scissors, to free the leaves of gold and tissue.

Slide your thumb and index finger over the cut edge, holding the edge at an angle. This takes out the crimping caused by the scissor blades and prevents the leaves of gold and tissue from sticking together.

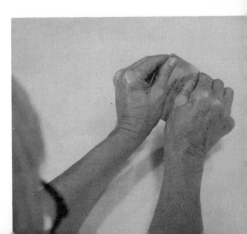

cut edge as it passes through your finger and thumb. This will prevent the cut edges of tissue from sticking to each other. Lay the book of leaf on a corner of the table where it will be accessible but will not be in the way of your work.

3. Use a new paring knife to lift off the thick paper cover from the book; beneath it will be a tissue covering the top leaf of gold. Now slip the knife under three or four leaves of tissue and gold, and lift them off, leaving a leaf of gold exposed on the book.

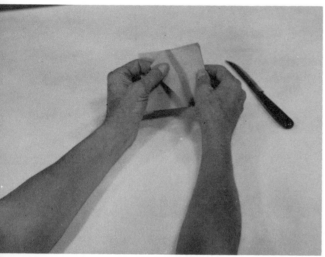

Lift the thick paper cover from the book.

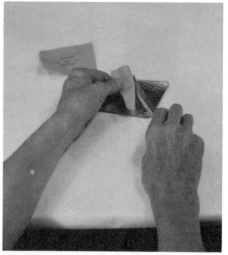

The knife will help you lift off a few leaves and tissues.

4. The gold leaves you removed from the book are protected by separating tissues. By aid of the paring knife pick them up from the table, gold and tissue, and hold them firmly with your fingers. Then, using the thumb and index finger of each hand, *tear* the leaves of gold and tissue into smaller pieces. *Do not cut them with scissors.* To do so would crimp the edges and cause the gold to stick to the tissues. Start at the top and tear slowly and evenly downward, about ¼ inch with each tearing motion. Reduce to desired sizes by first tearing the full-size leaves in half, then tearing each half in half, and so on.

Start at the top to tear the leaves in half.

Tear the leaves slowly and evenly, about ¼ inch with each motion. The tissues, top and bottom, will protect the fragile gold leaf from your fingers.

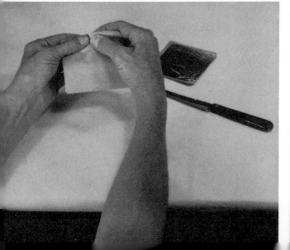

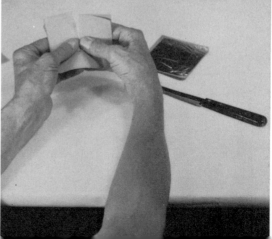

5. Move the small stacks of leaf to a place on the table near the object to be gilded. You can handle them easily by slipping the knife under the bottom tissue and picking up the stack between thumb and index finger. The leaf will not be damaged if your fingers touch only the tissues.

6. When you are ready to apply the leaf, use the knife to remove the top tissue from each stack, thus exposing the gold. Lift the tissue with the knife point and pick it off with thumb and index finger. If the knife should slide under several leaves and expose another tissue instead of gold, lift them off anyhow and turn them bottom side up so the gold will be on top. Repeat the removal of tissues as you apply the leaf. When the torn supply is exhausted, tear a fresh batch from the partially used book you have placed at a side of the table.

Tear the leaves to the sizes required, and place the stacks of leaves on the table. Cover the exposed leaf of gold on the book with a tissue, to keep it from blowing away.

4

Applying Gold Leaf

Two different techniques are required in applying leaf to (1) *parts to be mat leafed* (now coated with shellac) and (2) *parts to be burnished* (now coated with red burnish size).

Mat leafing is a simple procedure. It consists of coating the shellacked parts with oil-type size, then laying the leaf after the size has become "tacky"—that is, before it has completely dried. Burnish leafing is more difficult and takes practice to master. However, it is advisable to do this part first. If the mat gilding is completed first, there is danger of marring it while leafing the parts to be burnished.

Applying Leaf to Parts to Be Burnished

Parts to be burnished now have a surfacing of red burnish size over a gesso foundation. When the burnish size is wetted it becomes adhesive, because the rabbit skin glue it contains is resoluble. When gold leaf is laid on the wetted surface, it stays. This application method is called *water gilding*. It is not hard to understand but it requires some precision, and the work will be slow until you acquire a dexterity that comes with practice.

Tools and Materials

First, see that your tools and materials are in readiness on the table near the frame. These are:

1. *Gold leaf*. Torn to required sizes.

2. *Paring knife.* For handling the leaf. Should be thin, lightweight, and well balanced. Start with a new knife and use it for this purpose only.

3. *Gilder's tip.* A thin, flat brush about 4 inches wide, of very fine hair held in place between two pieces of cardboard. Used to pick up the leaf and transfer it to the object. The 4-inch brush is too wide for most uses; cut it in half with a pair of scissors to make two brushes.

4. *Round, sable, watercolor brush.* Size #12. For wetting the burnish size.

5. *Camel hair lettering quill.* Size #12. For pressing applied leaf into contact.

6. *Oval or round camel hair dusting brush.* Size ¾ inch. For brushing off loose edges of leaf.

7. *Cup containing alcohol solution.* At one time called "gilder's liquor." Used to wet the burnish size. Make the solution by mixing 7 teaspoons of distilled water and 3 teaspoons of denatured alcohol. Use a recognized brand of alcohol, such as Solux; do not use rubbing alcohol.

8. *Cup containing clear water.* Tap water will do. Used to rinse the sable brush. Place a clean washcloth next to the cup, to dry the brush.

Laying Leaf on Burnish Size

Gold leaf is applied to burnish size in a *5-step cycle* that is repeated with each piece of leaf. After some practice, you should go through the motions as automatically as you drive your car. Follow these steps:

First step. Take the gilder's tip in your right hand and brush it lightly across your hair to magnetize it. Pick up a piece of leaf by laying the edge of the tip over about ¼ inch (or less) of the edge of the leaf, and lifting. Transfer the tip, with the leaf hanging, to your left hand and hold it near the spot on the frame where you intend to lay it.

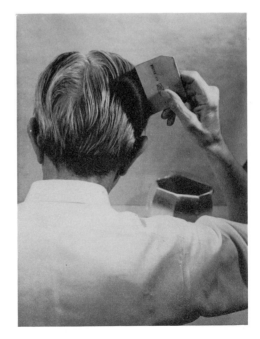

Magnetize the gilder's tip by brushing it lightly across your hair; give it several strokes. This must be done each time you pick up a piece of leaf. Instead of the hair, the tip may be brushed over a trouser leg or skirt.

To pick up a piece of leaf, lay the gilder's tip about ¼ inch over its edge
and gently lift it.

Unless you are ambidextrous, transfer the tip, with the leaf, to your left hand.

Second step. Take the round sable brush in your right hand and dip it in
the cup of alcohol solution. Then quickly brush the solution freely onto the
spot where the leaf is to be placed. Make it thoroughly wet, but do not press
hard or restroke with the brush. If the place dries before you can get the leaf
on it, pass it by and repeat the procedure later when it is *thoroughly* dry. If
you rewet a damp surface, you may wash away the red size.

Dip the brush in the alcohol solution . . .

. . . and brush the solution freely onto the spot where the leaf is to be laid.

USE YOUR OWN STYLE

The basic principles of gold leafing have been discovered over a long time by much trial and error. The principles must be followed—*but there are no set ways in which you must follow them.* To accomplish any of the established requirements you may use your right hand or your left, or change from one to the other. You may hold a brush at the middle or near the tip, and make the strokes long or short. You may improvise your own methods for any given procedure. The way that is easiest and most natural for *you* is the correct way—as long as it accomplishes the desired result. This is true of almost all artistic pursuits.

Third step. Within a few seconds—before the wet size can dry—lay in place the piece of leaf that is clinging to the gilder's tip in your left hand. If you are very right-handed, you may need to lay down the brush and transfer the tip with the leaf to your right hand, and so apply it—but it must be done quickly, while the size is still wet.

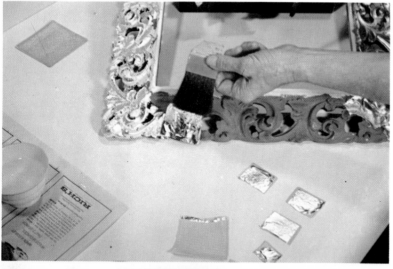

After wetting a spot, quickly lay the leaf over it.

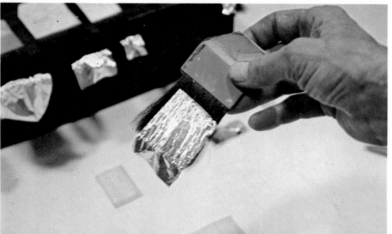

The wrong way to pick up a piece of leaf; the tip should touch only a narrow edge.

If the leaf should fall from the tip before you can lay it in place, try quickly to brush the tip over your hair, pick up another piece of leaf from the table, and cover the spot before it dries. If you don't make it in time, *do not rewet the spot*. Go back later after it has fully dried, then rewet and cover it. Some gilders anticipate such a mishap by having a few pieces of leaf hanging on tips, in readiness.

The way you handle the gilder's tip at the instant of application is very important and a little tricky. The leaf should be made to fall almost flat on the wet surface, in one quick motion. If the motion is slow and the bottom edge of the leaf touches the surface first, the leaf may tear.

The motion of the tip should be *over, down, and away*, in one stroke, leaving the leaf in place. The wet surface will snap it into contact. You may practice this motion by holding a piece of toilet tissue vertically in your fingers at the left side of a book, and then laying the tissue *over and flat down* on the book, releasing your fingers just as it touches the book.

As an insurance for covering wetted spots before they dry, you may place a box on the table . . .

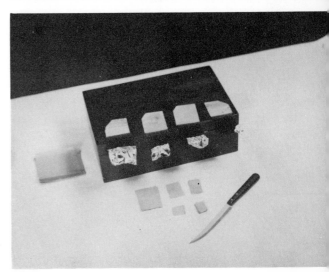

. . . to hold gilder's tips with leaf in readiness for quick application.

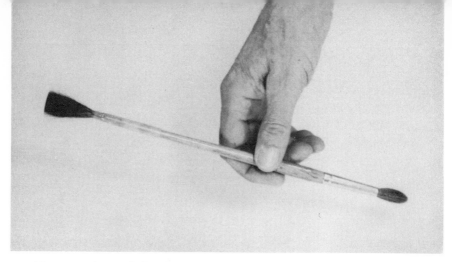

A gilder's pencil is made by slipping a camel-hair quill on the handle of the brush used to wet the burnish size. The quill end is used to quickly touch down the leaf after it has been laid in place. The gilder's tip can serve the same purpose.

Fourth step. Immediately after laying a piece of leaf, use the camel hair quill to gently touch down any parts that have not made full contact with the surface. You can slip the quill over the handle of the round sable brush, making what is called a "gilder's pencil." This can be twisted around in the same hand and serve as two brushes—one for wetting and one for pressing into contact. Some gilders use the gilder's tip for this purpose, which is more convenient, but the tip must not be allowed to touch the wet size.

Fifth Step. After laying *each* piece of leaf, rinse the sable brush in the cup of clear water; then squeeze out the water with the washcloth. This removes traces of size that are on the hairs after they have wetted a sized surface. If the brush is not rinsed it will contaminate the alcohol solution, and may leave a dulling film when it touches the edges of leaf already applied. Rinse the brush each time you apply a piece of leaf; change the water often.

After laying each piece of leaf, rinse the brush in clear water . . .

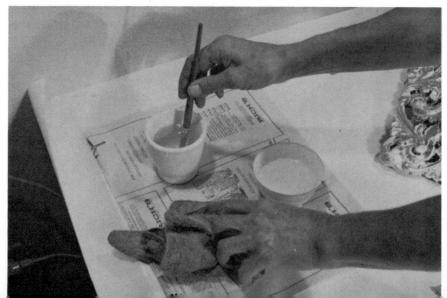

... then squeeze it damp-dry with the washcloth.

Some Precautions

Lay the leaf from the top of an object downward. If possible, place the object on the table at an incline so excess wetness will run off and not make puddles.

If a drop of alcohol solution becomes trapped under the leaf, a few sharp puffs of air from your lips may blow it out. Do not try to press it out with the brush or tip.

Avoid frequent rewettings; several rewettings of the same spot may cause the size to lose its adhesiveness.

Do not touch a dry, sized surface with wet or damp fingers; do not touch a *wet* sized surface with anything except the leaf.

When you have completely gilded the parts to be burnished, brush them lightly with the camel hair dusting brush to remove loose particles of leaf. This will disclose bare spots where the leaf did not adhere, which you now must patch. It's good economy to save the flakes of gold for future use; brush them into a small jar.

Patching

Both small and large bare spots may appear after you have brushed the surface free of loose gold leaf. Start at the top of the frame and cover these spots. The application procedure is the same, with these exceptions:

1. Tear the leaf in smaller pieces.

2. Prepare a weaker alcohol solution, in the proportion of only 1 teaspoon of alcohol in 7 teaspoons of distilled water. You cannot prevent the alcohol from getting on the edges of leaf already applied, and alcohol has a dulling effect on leaf that is to be burnished.

3. Do not wet the bare spots so freely that the solution runs onto leafed areas. Control the amount of solution by the depth you dip the brush in the cup.

4. To save time and motion in covering small spots: hold the tip with the

Bare spots in the hollows of carvings may be touched up with liquid gilt after the frame has been burnished.

leaf in your left hand directly over the spot; wet the spot with a quick stroke of the brush in your right hand; then lay the leaf, and touch it down with the gilder's tip.

5. A few bare spots may refuse to hold the leaf. If so, touch them with more burnish size, allow it to dry, and again apply leaf.

6. Disregard small, inaccessible spots in the hollows of carved ornaments and borders. You can cover these easily with liquid gilt after the burnishing is completed.

When all reachable places are covered with leaf, the burnish-gilded parts of the frame will be ready for you to burnish with an agate burnisher.

Some gilders apply all the leaf, both burnish leaf and mat leaf, before using the agate burnisher. If you prefer to do this, proceed with the following instructions for mat leafing. However, there is some danger of marring mat-leafed surfaces in handling during the burnishing process. You can avoid this by burnishing first, then laying the mat leaf. If you follow this safer course, proceed with the instructions for *Burnishing Gold Leaf*, p. 49, and then lay the mat leaf.

Applying Leaf to Parts to Be Mat Leafed

Gilding surfaces that are not to be burnished (mat leafing) is a simple matter of brushing on an adhesive size and laying the leaf over it. Two kinds of sizes may be used—*quick drying* and *slow drying;* and two forms of gold leaf—*loose packed* and *patent.*

On the frame we are gilding, parts to be burnished are now leafed. The next step can be either to burnish these parts or to lay the mat leaf. This is optional, so we shall proceed with the mat leafing.

Smoothing the Surface

The areas to be mat leafed are now coated with shellac. Rub them with 4/0 steel wool to remove brush marks. It is seldom advisable to use finishing paper because it may cut through the shellac to the porous gesso foundation. Brush and wipe the object free of dust.

Shellacked surfaces are smoothed by rubbing them with 4/0 steel wool.

Applying Oil-type Size

Always work in a warm, dust-free room. If the outer edges of a frame or liner are to be sized, place a few small blocks of wood under it so the brush will not drag size over the top of the worktable. Then:

1. Pour a small quantity of quick-drying, oil-type size into a cup or other small container. Apply it like varnish with a suitably sized flat sable brush. A ⅝-inch brush will serve most purposes; use a smaller or larger width where required. You may need a very narrow brush to dab the size into deep recesses and undercuts. Apply the size thinly and evenly, brushing in one direction.

Oil-type size is poured into a cup for application.

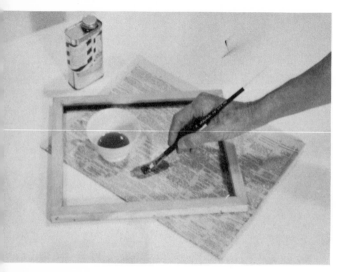

When you first dip the brush, stroke the excess load of size onto a piece of paper. This prevents the first stroke on the object from leaving too much size.

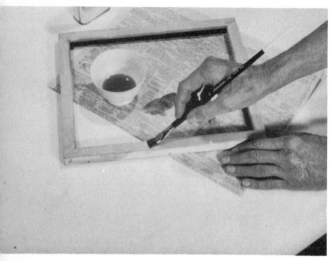

A sable brush does the smoothest job. Apply the size thinly and evenly.

2. Size only as large an area as you can cover with leaf in an hour. If you size more, the surface may become entirely dry before you can leaf it.

3. When the size has become sufficiently tacky it is ready to receive the leaf. This usually takes from 1 to 2 hours. After 1 hour, test it by placing a knuckle firmly against the sized surface and then quickly pulling it away. If you hear a crisp "click" or "tick," the size is ready; if the surface feels wet or if some size clings to your knuckle, test it again in half an hour.

Test the size by placing a knuckle firmly against the surface, then quickly pulling it away. A crisp "click" tells that the size is ready.

Laying Leaf on Oil-type Size

Lay the leaf promptly when the size has reached the right tack. If the leafing takes too long, the size will harden and the leaf will not adhere to it.

You may apply either loose-packed or patent leaf over oil-type size. Patent leaf is very convenient for gilding flat, smooth surfaces. Only loose-packed leaf can be used on carved, embossed, or undercut areas. Many gilders prefer to use the loose-packed leaf on all surfaces.

Applying Loose-packed Leaf

You will need a book of leaf, the camel hair dusting brush, paring knife, and gilder's tip. Proceed as follows:

1. Tear a number of gold leaves to required sizes and place them on the table as you did when leafing the burnish-sized parts of the frame. If you

are leafing a long, narrow side, the pieces of leaf should be torn about ¼ inch wider than the side, so the leaf will overlap the outer edge of the frame. For a large surface it may be best to tear the full-size leaves into quarters. After some practice you will be able to cover large areas with full-size leaves, using a full-size gilder's tip.

2. Pick up the pieces of leaf with the tip and lay them on the surface one at a time, overlapping about ⅛ inch. Gently touch them down with the tip, but do not let the tip—or your fingers—touch the tacky size. On carved and recessed parts of ornaments, use narrow pieces of leaf; lower them vertically, like a ribbon, into the depressions. Several pieces of leaf may be required to cover a hard-to-reach spot. If you have saved some gold flake brushings, dab them into the hollows.

3. When the sized surface has been entirely leafed, press the leaf down gently with the *side* of the camel hair dusting brush. Then brush the surface very lightly to loosen clinging edges of overlapped leaf. If uncovered spots appear, brush the particles of leaf over them; the particles should adhere. Cover large bare spots with fresh leaf from the table.

4. Put the mat-leafed parts of the frame aside and do not touch them for at least 12 hours. Then rub the surfaces briskly but gently with absorbent cotton which you can purchase at a drugstore; do not use coarse, commercial cotton. Be careful when handling mat-leafed parts. Oil-type size hardens slowly, and for several weeks the surfaces will be very susceptible to scratching.

Caution: Never use an agate burnisher on a surface that has been gilded over oil-type size.

Applying Patent Leaf

This form of gold leaf can be handled with the fingers. It can be applied effectively to flat surfaces, concave channels, and rounded convex columns. The procedure is easy, as follows:

1. Open a book of patent leaf. With the aid of the knife, remove several leaves of gold with their tissue backings and place them, gold side up, on the table. Try to touch only the back or margin of the tissues with your fingers.

When you use patent leaf, it is not necessary to cut off the binding edge of the book. Tissues holding the leaf slip easily out of the opened book.

The knife will enable you to handle the tissues without your fingers touching the gold.

2. Cut the leaves into required sizes with a sharp pair of scissors, and place the cut pieces near the frame or liner you are gilding. Under normal conditions, patent leaf will not separate from its tissue backing when cut with sharp scissors and handled gently. However, it will separate if you try to tear it.

3. Test the size with your knuckle, as described for loose-packed leaf.

4. To apply a piece of patent leaf, slide the knife under it, lift up an edge, and pick it up by the tissue margin with your fingers. Lay the gold side down over the sized surface. Then rub a finger flatly over the entire surface of the tissue, to press the leaf into contact. Lift the tissue off the leaf with the point of the knife. Allow each piece of leaf to overlap the preceding piece by about ⅛ inch.

Patent leaf can be cut to required sizes with sharp scissors, and can be transferred to the object with fingers and knife.

Lay the gold side down over the sized surface . . .

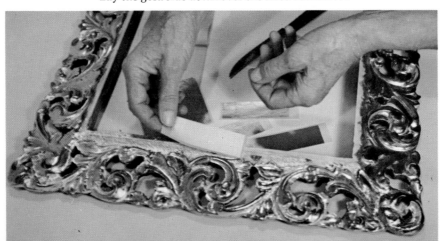

. . . then press it down firmly with your fingers.

Patent leaf is easily applied to smooth, flat surfaces.

5. After you have covered the surface, there may be some almost imperceptible breaks in the leaf that would show up later. Guard against this by pressing a fresh, full-size leaf against the gilded surface, lifting it up and laying it down until it has come in contact with the entire gilded area. This will cover tiny holes and cracks.

5

Burnishing Gold Leaf

AFTER GILDING A SURFACE, WAIT AT LEAST SEVERAL HOURS BEFORE BURNISHING IT. You may wait for a number of days, but do not delay this step longer than is necessary. Best effects are achieved when burnishing is done before the dampened burnish size has fully hardened beneath its gold-leaf cover.

To *burnish* means to make shiny or lustrous. Today, as for centuries past, whenever the word is used it brings to mind *gold*. This metal, more than any other art medium, is brought to its fullest beauty by burnishing.

Gold that is laid over oil-type size can be made more lustrous by rubbing the surface with refined absorbent cotton, but this is not true burnishing. Gold-leaf burnishing must be done with an agate burnisher. This tool consists of a polished agate tip fastened to a wooden handle. Other materials may be used—many years ago, gilders used a dog's tooth—but the agate is recognized as best.

Agate Burnishing Tools

Agate burnishers are available in a variety of sizes and shapes designed to reach different kinds of places on an object. To burnish most frames and other art objects you may get by with only a medium-size and possibly a small-size curved burnisher. It will be convenient if you have at hand a few other sizes and shapes. Which ones to use for different surfaces will soon become apparent when you get into the work.

You will find that the general-purpose curved agate is ingeniously shaped so you may twist it in your fingers to reach different curves and angles.

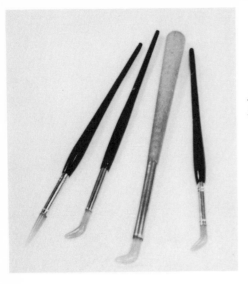

Agate burnishers are made in different sizes and shapes.

The curved agate burnisher is designed to reach different contours and angles.

The broad, flat part of the agate is best for flat areas; the extreme tip reaches narrow and deep places.

Agate burnishing can be done only to leaf that has been laid over a size especially prepared for burnish work. Directions given here apply to the treatment of leaf laid over a clay-type size. *Do not use an agate to burnish leaf laid over any other kind of size unless the size manufacturer specifically recommends it.*

Using the Agate Burnisher

Burnishing is slow, but it is easy, and the results are very rewarding. Follow these directions:

Grasp the handle of the burnisher near the tip, as you would a pencil. Rub the broad curve of the agate back and forth in left-to-right strokes, exerting a moderately hard pressure. The hand motion is sideways from the wrist, and the strokes are an inch or less wide.

Let the stroking motion travel slowly over the surface, from top to bottom or from left to right. If dull lines show between the shiny strokes, it indicates that you are trying to carry the work ahead too rapidly—that is, making too few strokes for the space covered; go back and rub out the dull lines.

A little practice will tell you how much pressure to put on the agate. If the pressure is too light, it will not produce the desired brilliance. If it is too heavy, or if the rubbing is too prolonged, it may rub off some of the leaf and the red size will show through. Take care not to press hard on sharp edges; the gesso foundation may chip if you do.

It is sometimes difficult to get a good burnished effect on large, flat areas. It may be advisable to burnish these in two stages: first, rub the entire surface with light pressure, moving the agate in vertical, horizontal, and circular strokes; second, go over the surface again, using straight-line strokes and increasing pressure to produce full, even brilliance.

Penciled lines show how the agate may be rubbed over a gilded surface in different motions.

Touching out small bare spots in hollows and crevices is done after an object has been completely leafed and burnished.

After you have burnished an object, go back and cover the small bare spots, where the leaf did not reach, in the hollows of carved and embossed ornaments. The easiest way is to use a liquid gilt, available in small bottles at art-supplies stores. Touch it lightly onto the spots with a size #1 round bristle brush. Do not apply this liquid before burnishing; it should not come in contact with the agate burnisher.

6

Gilding with Composition Leaf and Bronzing Powders

MOST OF THE "GOLD-LEAFED" OBJECTS MANUFACTURED TODAY ARE COATED WITH gold-colored metal alloys. These materials are applied in three forms—leaf, powder, and liquid. Composition leaf is imitation gold leaf; it is also called Dutch metal leaf. Bronzing powders are also composed of metal alloys, very finely powdered; they contain no real gold. Liquid gilt is bronzing powder in a varnishlike base. All three forms are available at art-supplies stores, in a variety of gold and bronze shades.

These base-metal substitutes are inexpensive and easy to handle. They can be used effectively on objects that do not merit the use of real gold. After being applied, they must be given protective coatings of lacquer, shellac, or varnish; else they will tarnish in a very short time.

Composition leaf and bronzing powders are often used in combination with genuine gold leaf. The powders are convenient for touching up deep recesses and hollows after an object has been leafed with real gold.

Applying Composition Leaf

Composition leaf is packaged in books of 25 leaves, like gold leaf, but the leaves are larger—5½ inches square. Composition leaf is many times as thick as gold leaf. It can be handled with the fingers, and it does not tear easily when cut with sharp scissors.

This leaf is laid over an oil-type adhesive size. It has a high luster that can be increased by rubbing it with absorbent cotton. The application pro-

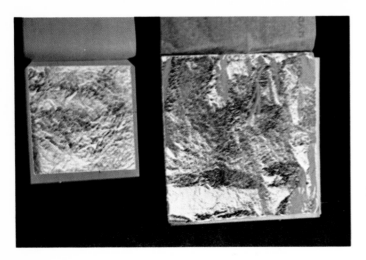

Opened books of: *left*, genuine gold leaf, and *right*, composition gold leaf. Both are loose packed, with separating tissues between the metal leaves. The composition leaves are much larger and thicker.

cedure is basically the same as for genuine gold leaf, with minor differences. Follow these steps:

1. Smooth the surface and seal it with shellac or varnish. A gesso foundation contributes to smoothness but is not essential. If you use gesso, apply shellac to seal it.

2. Apply an oil-type size, either quick- or slow-drying. Sizes made especially for the thicker metal leaves (aluminum, copper, composition) are available, but the regular gold size is quite satisfactory if the leaf is applied carefully. Be sure the surface is thoroughly covered with size. Lay the composition leaf when the size reaches a distinct "tack," but do not wait quite as long as you would for gold leaf.

3. Use sharp scissors to cut the leaf. First cut off the binding edge of the book to lift off half a dozen metal leaves with their separating tissues. Cut them to the required sizes and "fan" them out on the table to facilitate handling.

4. Use the knife and your fingers to pick up a piece of leaf and its tissue. Lay the leaf on the sized surface with the tissue on top; press it into contact with your fingers. Continue laying pieces of leaf, allowing overlaps, until the entire surface is covered. Remove the tissues as you go along.

To facilitate handling, composition leaves are fanned out, like a deck of playing cards. The fanned out leaves and tissues are easy to pick up with knife and fingers.

5. Go over the surface again and lay pieces of leaf over all *possible* places where there may be breaks or cracks in the leaf just laid. Some gilders put a double layer of leaf over the surface, to take no chances. It is better to lose some of the inexpensive leaf than to go back and patch a lot of bare spots that might show up.

6. The leaf now must be pressed *very firmly* into contact with the sized surface. Because of its thickness, composition leaf does not adhere as readily as real gold leaf.

Press and rub the leaf against the surface, *always keeping a piece of tissue between your fingers and the leaf*. If the tissue sticks in places, it indicates that an unnoticed crack or break has not been covered.

Give extra attention to the corners and edges of moldings. You may need to slide a fingernail along sharp-angled joinings in order to make firm contact.

7. Do not attempt to cover small recesses and hollows of carvings with composition leaf. Use liquid gilt, or a matching shade of bronzing powder that can be easily dusted into them; do this after the leafing is completed.

8. Allow the work to dry and harden overnight; then rub off excess leaf with absorbent cotton. If some bare spots now appear, patch them with size and leaf.

Surfaces covered with composition leaf must be given one or more transparent protective coatings to retard tarnishing. Metal lacquers for this purpose are sold by suppliers of gilding materials. Some gilders use thinned white shellac—about 1 part denatured alcohol to 2 parts shellac. A more durable coating, and easier to apply smoothly, is the quick-drying, oil-type gold size.

Any kind of coating will have a dulling effect on a metallic surface. Lacquer or shellac may be applied safely to a leafed surface if the adhesive size used to hold the leaf has thoroughly dried; they may "lift" the leaf from the surface if the size has not dried hard. It is advisable to let a newly leafed object stand for several days or more; then test the coating material on a small spot before applying.

Applying Bronzing Powders

Bronzing powders are made of pulverized metal. They are available in many shades of gold, silver, bronze, and other colors. Manufacturers provide color charts from which you may make selections.

These powders may be used to gild an entire object or parts of an object, and to highlight ornaments, produce antique patinas, cover bare spots, and blend-in scars and patches.

When you apply bronzing powder, prepare the surface exactly as described for composition leaf. Quick-drying gold size is an excellent adhesive for the powder. Here are a few guiding points:

1. Allow the size to reach a tack not quite as sharp as for gold leaf.

2. You may be able to purchase the exact color from the wide range of available shades. If not, mix different shades of powder to get the desired color.

Bronzing powders are sold in small, plastic containers. Larger quantities in cans are more economical.

3. Dust the powder plentifully over the tacky size; use a ¾-inch oval or round camel hair dusting brush. Keep the brush well filled with powder, and *let the hairs hardly touch the tacky surface.* If the brush is well filled and you do not pause in your brushing strokes, the size will hold the powder and will not get on the brush. Make sure all corners and crevices are covered.

Bronzing powder may be applied to a sized surface with a cheesecloth pad instead of a brush, but sometimes this method does not produce an even finish.

4. To cover bare recesses in carved ornaments, size the places and push the powder into them with a narrow brush. Liquid gilt is sometimes more convenient for this purpose.

5. Let the object stand at least 12 hours for the size to harden. *Do not touch dusted parts with your fingers:* they would leave prints.

6. Brush off excess powder with a feather duster, or blow it off with a reversed vacuum cleaner. All loose powder must be removed without scratching the surface. Finish by wiping the surface with a clean flannel cloth.

7. Areas gilded with a bronzing powder must be given a tarnish-retarding coating, as described for imitation gold leaf. First, however, it is necessary to "set" the gilded surface with a *spray*—do not use a brush. Use a clear, acrylic spray, sold by all art-supplies stores. Then *brush on* one coat of white, thinned shellac.

Articles that are handled in frequent use, such as chairs, tables, cabinets, and boxes, should be given additional coats of clear, tough varnish.

Using Liquid Gilt

You may buy liquid gilt ready-mixed, or you may mix your own. These coatings are metallic paints composed of bronzing powders in varnishlike liquids. They are the easiest gilding mediums to apply, but give the least pleasing effects when used on large areas. However, they are very convenient —and satisfactory—for *some* gilding purposes.

To make a liquid gilt, simply mix bronzing powder in any of a number of suitable base vehicles—banana liquid, clear varnish, quick-drying gold size, or one of the specially prepared liquids sold by art-supplies stores. The proportions vary—1 part powder to 3, 4, or 5 parts liquid, by volume. Usually it is more practical to buy ready-mixed liquid gilt.

Gilders find liquid gilt most useful for covering small, deep hollows and other hard-to-reach spots that remain bare after an object has been gilded with either genuine or imitation gold leaf. It is also handy for quickly coating large surfaces when brilliance and permanence are not essential but low cost is.

Surfaces coated with liquid gilt should receive a tarnish-retarding coat of clear shellac or varnish.

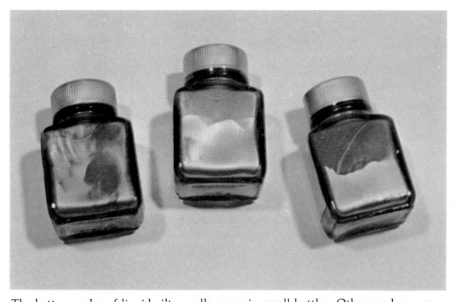

The better grades of liquid gilt usually come in small bottles. Other grades, sometimes labeled "metallic gold paint," are sold in larger cans for various commercial purposes.

7

Antiquing

ONE OF THE MOST CONTROVERSIAL QUESTIONS ABOUT ANTIQUES IS *how far should restoration be carried?* It may be well to consider this before starting to antique a newly gilded object.

To "antique" once meant to simulate the marks left by time and use. Today it more often means to fake or preserve *damage* caused by neglect and abuse. Some antiques fanciers will not glance twice at a piece that has been restored to a presentable condition. There is widespread belief that an antique should have a beaten-up appearance.

We can only guess at the origins of this notion. Of course, over the years, many owners have been sentimentally disinclined to have their antique heirlooms repaired or changed in any way. Friends and visitors who saw these antiques in the homes noted that they were old and dilapidated and *valuable.* The three qualities seemed to go together. A state of disrepair came to be considered an essential characteristic of a worthwhile antique.

But the chief reason so many antiques are unsightly is, probably, the scarcity of skilled restorers. Today the average antiques dealer has difficulty finding a cabinetmaker experienced in this field. Carvers and gilders are few and far between. It follows that a large percentage of antiques in retail shops need restoration of one kind or another. Customers expect this, and many look with suspicion on an antique in fine condition.

On the other hand, there are owners and collectors who want their antiques to be in perfect condition. It appears that the early owners did. Labels on mirror frames of eighteenth century makers carried advertising inscriptions such as "Old Picture Frames Regilt," and "Looking Glasses New Quicksilvered." These services were offered in response to a demand, so we must conclude that discriminating owners of that day did not want shabby furnishings in their homes.

And it is interesting to see that many of the handsomely restored antiques at Williamsburg and in the Winterthur Museum look almost new. So do many of the restored articles offered for sale by the highest-priced antiques dealers in the United States and England.

Regardless of how lightly or heavily you decide to antique a gilded object, the procedure is the same. It consists of shading and darkening the low, recessed places, and possibly rubbing or painting artificial "wear" on some raised surfaces. Low places on gilded objects darken naturally through the years by accumulating a film from the dust, oil, smoke, and other microscopic particles in the air. Raised surfaces show wear from handling and cleaning. The resultant contrast of light and dark, and the metallic gleam of gold, makes the warm patina that gives gilded antiques their unique charm. Your challenge is to compete with nature and apply the antiquing so it will not be obviously artificial.

Antiquing Materials and Methods

Many coloring materials, liquid and dry, can be used as antiquing mediums. Semitransparent liquids are preferred because they allow the gold to glint dimly through the darkened surface. Two kinds are recommended— *varnish base* and *shellac base*. Varnish-base liquids usually are colored with oil pigments and they dry slowly, in from 12 to 36 hours. Shellac-base liquids may be colored with soluble stains, or they may consist of shellac to which has been added insoluble dry coloring which must be stirred during application. These dry within a few hours.

Varnish-base Liquids

An easy way to darken small recesses and hollows is to paint them with a good grade of *varnish stain*, sold at all paint stores. Dark walnut is the most suitable antiquing color. A little rottenstone powder may be added to gray the coloring and kill the varnish gloss.

Antiquing colors most often used are blends of burnt umber, raw umber, Vandyke brown, Venetian red, and yellow ocher. You may blend these colorings to produce the shade you want, and add them to an eggshell or semigloss furniture varnish. Artists' oil colors, sold by all art-supplies stores, may be used. When they are added to varnish, the drying time may be greatly increased. *It is advisable to test any antiquing preparation before applying it.*

A brand of general-purpose colorants trade-named Tints-All may be added to furniture varnish with little effect on drying time. It is sold in tubes in paint stores, in all the antiquing colors. (See *Gilding Supplies*, p. 108.)

Shellac-base Liquids

The only advantage of shellac as a base for antiquing is that it dries quickly. Shades and depths of color may be built up by numerous coats without a long wait for each to dry. Colored shellac is not recommended for toning large areas because it is difficult to apply without leaving streaks or brush marks. However, white shellac or thinned orange shellac is excellent for this use.

You can color shellac the same way as varnish, except that the coloring additive must be soluble in alcohol. Aniline dyes can be used. They are sold in dry form and must be dissolved in alcohol and added to the shellac. However, the anilines do not include the colors needed for good antiquing, and these dyes are not readily available at retail in most cities.

The most practical shellac-base liquid is a mixture of white shellac and *dry pigment colors*. Pour some thinned shellac into a small, capped jar; add dry pigment colors to produce the shade you need; thin the mixture with a little alcohol. The dry pigments are sold by art-supplies stores in all the antiquing colors. When mixed in a liquid, they must be stirred during use.

Applying an Antiquing Varnish

To apply the varnish, shake or stir the container and pour some into a small receptacle such as a jar top. Add a few drops of turpentine if the varnish starts to thicken as you work. Apply it with a narrow, flat sable brush; sizes from #2 to #6 should be suitable for corners, recesses, hollows, and other hard-to-reach places.

To achieve a natural effect, apply the varnish very thinly with a "half-dry" brush. (Each time you dip the brush into the varnish, draw it lightly over a piece of paper to thin its load.)

It may take three or four applications to arrive at a natural shading and color depth. The first coat should be quite faint. Each successive coat may be spotted over only parts of the preceding coats in order to produce shading and deeper darkening where needed. Allow each coat to dry thoroughly before applying the next.

Precaution: If you have used liquid gilt to cover bare spots on the places you intend to antique, touch these places with shellac first; otherwise the antiquing varnish may soften the gilt.

Applying an Antiquing Shellac

If you are using plain white or orange shellac for large, smooth areas, thin it with 1 part alcohol to 2 parts shellac. Work quickly; do not let the brush start to dry between strokes; and avoid restroking.

If dry pigment colors have been added to the shellac, follow the same procedure as for applying antiquing varnish, *except that you must use alcohol, not turpentine, as a solvent.*

Shellac dries rapidly; successive coats may be applied at intervals of 2 or 3 hours. After the first coat, care must be taken not to let the brush strokes hesitate on the surface. Make the strokes light and quick to avoid softening and smearing the underlying coats.

Antiquing with Dry Pigment Colors

Dry pigments are useful chiefly for accenting hollows where greater darkening is desired and transparency is not. Usually these powders should not be applied to other parts of an object, except to touch up damage scars. Their function is to *cover*, and they obscure whatever lies beneath.

Dry pigments are best applied with shellac as a binder. Use a narrow, flat bristle brush. Choose your colors and pour a little of each colored powder in a separate pile in a saucer. Then pour a little thinned shellac into a small container, or into the center of the saucer. Dip the brush in the shellac, press it into some powder, and quickly apply it.

By keeping the brush wet with shellac, you can use the saucer as a palette and stir the colors together to make the desired shade. Metallic bronzing powders may be combined with the dry pigments.

Have at hand a glass containing alcohol in which to dip the brush if the shellac becomes gummy on the saucer.

This weather-beaten Buddha is having some of its lost gilt restored. It must be antiqued to look severely but naturally timeworn. Gold leaf and enamel will be applied, and then "distressed"—that is, rubbed off in places.

The first step is to apply a coating of thinned shellac to which has been added a little raw umber dry pigment and rottenstone.

Gold leaf is spotted on the figure, over oil-type size, and then rubbed lightly with steel wool to simulate wear.

Shading, blending, and "aging" is done with dry pigment colors, applied with a shellac binder. Then steel wool is used again to dull unseemly gloss.

The Buddha has taken on an aura of timeless veneration.

Antiquing Raised Surfaces

Usually it is not desirable to antique large, flat areas or smooth, raised surfaces of panels, columns, moldings, ornaments, and borders. However, if a faint darkening is desired you may apply the antiquing varnish described on page 60. Thin it with turpentine to the desired color depth, and test it before applying.

If you wish to dull the brilliance of raised surfaces very slightly, apply a coat of white shellac thinned with an equal volume of alcohol.

Wear may be simulated on a mat-gilded surface by rubbing it very lightly with 4/0 steel wool. This should be done before applying an antiquing liquid, and only to surfaces that have been given a brownish or red brown undercoat before the leaf was applied (see *Colored Gesso*, p. 20). Burnished surfaces may be treated in the same way; they already have a red or yellow clay undercoating. The steel wool should be used with almost a feather touch. Rub only until the faintest suggestion of dullness shows through the leaf.

The Frame Completed

When you reach this point your frame is repaired, gilded, antiqued, and ready to grace a picture or mirror. The next project you undertake may be gilding a clock, chair, table, or other object that gold leaf can beautify. The same basic steps and principles that you have followed will apply, with minor adaptations, to other objects, as explained on following pages. Be encouraged by knowing that your future gilding will be easier and better as you continue.

A final thought for the frame: if you put a mirror in it, first paint the *inside* of the frame's holding flange with liquid gilt; a mirror reflects the inner surface of this flange.

The completed frame.

8

How to Make a Mold and Casting

When an ornament is missing from an object, it can be replaced if an identical ornament is left intact. On a symmetrically designed frame, for example, an ornament missing from the top right-hand corner can be replaced by making a mold and casting of a duplicate ornament on the bottom left-hand corner.

To make a casting (which is the replacement) you first must make a mold. This is done by pressing, pouring, or painting a soft material over the model ornament and into its carved depressions. When the material hardens it is lifted off, and is then the mold.

Several kinds of mold-making materials may be purchased at art-supplies stores, ceramics shops, or from the manufacturers. The kind of material you use must depend on whether or not the ornament is *undercut*.

An ornament is undercut when some of its carved surfaces turn inward, making them smaller at the bottom than at the top. The mold, then, must be made of a pliant or elastic material, like rubber, so its bottom edges will stretch when it is pulled off over the wider top edges. If a rigid, nonelastic material is used for an undercut ornament, the mold cannot be removed from the model after it hardens.

On an ornament that has no undercutting, the carved surfaces are wider at the bottom than at the top. For this ornament you can make an *impression mold*, using a material that is not elastic. After the material has hardened on the ornament, it can be lifted off without being stretched.

There are many ways to make a mold and casting of an ornament when there is a duplicate ornament to serve as a model. We shall describe several methods:

Making a Nonelastic Impression Mold

An impression mold is the quickest and easiest to make. The method described here can be used only for ornaments that are not undercut. The
material used is *base plate wax,* available from dental-supplies dealers. It
comes in thin sheets measuring 1/16" × 2¾" × 5¾". Dentists use it to make
impression molds for dentures. It is especially useful in making molds of
thin, embossed bands and borders, and of ornaments that are not very
deeply carved.

Make the mold as follows:

1. Fill a saucepan with hot water—too hot to hold your fingers in com-
fortably, but not steaming. Place a sheet of the wax in the water and push it
under with your fingers. Let it stay 15 to 30 seconds until it is soft and pliable.

Dental base plate wax is softened by immersing it in hot water.

2. Remove the wax from the water and place it immediately over the
model ornament. Then work quickly, before the wax hardens. Press it tightly
around the edges of the ornament and into the carved depressions. Press with
the tips of your fingers—but not your fingernails; they would cut through
the soft wax. Use the eraser end of a pencil, or a similar object, to press the
wax into small hollows.

3. As the wax begins to harden, lift it gently and evenly around the edges
until it snaps loose from the ornament. Then dip it into cold water and you
will have a hard, brittle mold. Handle it carefully to prevent breaking.

The soft wax is pressed into conformation with the carved surface of the model ornament.

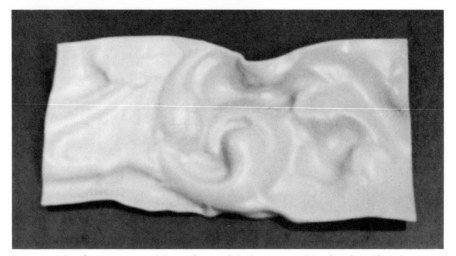

After being removed from the model, the wax mold is hard and brittle.

Making an Elastic Mold

Liquid mold rubber can be used to reproduce almost any kind of ornament. It is especially suitable for undercut carvings because it is elastic after it hardens and can easily be removed from recessed parts of the model. It has the disadvantage of requiring a number of days to make, but the finished mold is sharp and accurate. It can be used for an indefinite number of castings. This is how to make it:

1. Clean the model ornament with alcohol and a small, stiff brush. If the recesses are clogged with paint, use paint remover.

A casting made from this rosette will replace a missing rosette on another corner of the frame.

2. Brush all surfaces of the model with a thin vegetable oil, such as Wesson oil, to facilitate later removal of the mold. Ceramics shops sell "separating liquid" for this use.

3. Use a narrow, flat bristle brush; apply a thin coat of liquid rubber to the entire surface of the model ornament. Make sure the rubber fills all indentations and hollows. Use the tip of the bristles to push it into place. It is not necessary for the coating to have a smooth top surface.

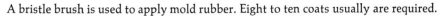

A bristle brush is used to apply mold rubber. Eight to ten coats usually are required.

4. Allow the first coat to dry overnight. Then apply five or six more coats at intervals of 10 or 12 hours, or longer.

5. Thicken some liquid rubber by mixing into it a fiber filler that is sold by rubber manufacturers and ceramics shops for this use. Mix to the consistency of a thick paste, and make two or three more applications to build up the mold and give it body. The repeated coatings should entirely fill in the carved design and cover it under a rubber blanket ¼ inch thick or more.

6. Allow the mold to "cure" on the model for several days. Then remove it slowly by lifting up the edges and pulling it off.

For the final coatings, the liquid rubber is poured into a cup and thickened with a fiber filler.

The filler is a fluffy material that gives body to the mold.

The mixture should have the consistency of a thick paste.

The fortified rubber mixture may be applied thickly. Two or three applications should be sufficient.

Allow the mold to remain on the model and "cure" for several days.

Loosen the mold gently from the undercut edges of the model.

The finished mold can be used to make many castings.

Other Mold-Making Materials and Methods

Most brands of mold-making materials are designed for molding sculptured figures or ceramic objects, or for other specialized purposes. Some, however, can be adapted to a gilder's restoration needs. It is well to get acquainted with what is available and to watch for new materials and processes as they are developed. A useful technique often turns up from an unlikely source.

Extremely accurate molds of undercut ornaments and intricate carvings can be made with *alginate impression powder*. This is sold under a number of trade names and is used by dentists to make mouth impressions for dentures.

Timing is important in the use of alginate powder. It must be mixed with water in a minute's time; poured over the ornament within another minute; and the gellike mold can be removed and cast a few minutes later. The mold can be used for only a single casting. The material is available from dental-supplies dealers.

Directions and measuring cups are provided with each container of alginate powder. First, the water is poured into a mixing bowl.

The powder is added to the water.

Mixing must be done very quickly. A rubber mixing bowl and stiff spatula are preferred but not essential.

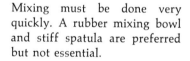

The mixed alginate is applied immediately to the model and worked into all hollows and crevices.

The alginate sets up into a gelatinous mass within a few minutes. Five minutes later, the mold may be removed from the model.

Some restorers make molds of thin, embossed ornaments by pressing a warmed cake of paraffin wax over them; some use a cake of soap. We know an antiques dealer who gets pretty good results with a child's molding composition trade-named Silly Putty. Of course, such molds can be made only of objects that are not undercut. If you should consider using any of these or similar methods, we suggest that you experiment with them first.

Making a Casting

Any pourable casting material can be used in the types of molds we have described. Plaster of paris is commonly used but it does not set up as strong as some other compounds, and it breaks easily in shaping if the casting is thin.

An inexpensive and easy-to-use product, trade-named Durham's Water Putty, is sold by hardware- and builders-supplies firms. This can be used also as a mending putty to fill large holes and replace areas of the original plaster foundation so often missing from old objects.

Many kinds of casting materials are sold by dealers in art and ceramics supplies. They also may be purchased directly from the manufacturers. Different products require different methods of mixing and pouring. Some are thin and some are thick; some harden in a few minutes and others require several hours or several days. It is important to follow directions on the container of the product you buy.

Filling the Mold

If you are filling a rubber mold, first brush it lightly with a thin vegetable oil or other separator to prevent the casting from sticking to the mold. Thin wax molds need no separation treatment. With molds made of other materials, follow the manufacturer's instruction.

Before filling the mold, place it on a flat, level surface. If necessary, put small pieces of wood under a low side or corner to level it so the casting mixture will not run out.

If the mixture flows freely, you may pour it directly from the mixing cup into the mold. Pour at one end or side of the mold and let the mixture find its way over the tops and into the depressions.

If the mixture is thick, like a heavy cake batter, it is better to "spoon" it into the mold. Care must be taken to prevent air from being trapped between the mixture and the mold. Feed the mixture into the mold at one spot—a side, corner, or the middle—and push it slowly along with the bottom of the spoon so it moves under its own gravity, like lava, into all crevices and hollows.

Molds to be filled are placed on a flat, level surface. Plaster-type casting compounds are mixed by adding the powder to water.

If the casting mixture is thick, spoon it into the mold.

Separating the Casting

To remove a wax mold, place it and the casting in hot water for about 30 seconds; then peel off the soft wax. Most wax molds cannot be reused.

A rubber mold is easily removed from the casting by stretching it loose from the undercut carving and pulling it off. The mold will spring back to its original shape and may be used for additional castings if needed.

Other types of molds should be removed as directed on the products' container labels.

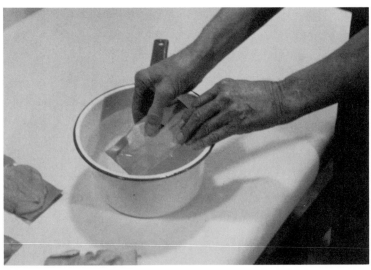

To remove a wax mold from the casting, place them in hot water until the wax softens.

Peel off the softened wax mold. It cannot be used again.

A rubber mold is removed by stretching it and pulling it off.

If the casting has thin edges, care must be taken not to break them when removing the mold. Most casting compounds require time to harden completely.

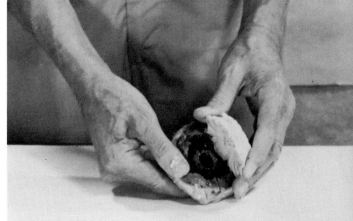

After the casting is removed, the rubber mold may be washed with soap and water and saved for possible future use.

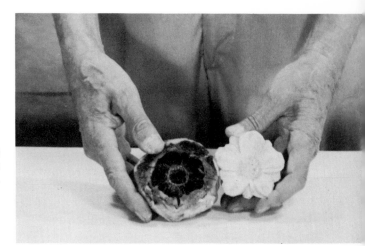

Fitting the Casting

The casting will be larger than the vacant space it is to fill. Saw or file it down to almost the required size. Then shape it as follows:

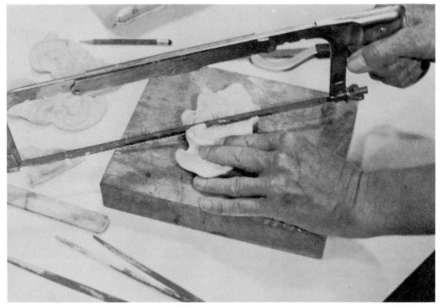

Excess plaster is sawed off before starting to trim and fit the new ornament.

1. Level the bottom surface by rubbing it back and forth over a full sheet of coarse (#80) sandpaper tacked onto a flat piece of wood. Continue rubbing until the casting has been reduced to the proper thickness. If it is much too thick, you can save time and effort by sawing off a slice with a fine-toothed saw. A hacksaw cuts casting plaster smoothly and evenly.

Thickness of the casting can be reduced by rubbing it on a full sheet of coarse sandpaper.

2. If the casting is to be glued to a convex surface, such as a half-round molding or column, you will need to hollow out the bottom of the casting to make it fit. This can be done with a convex rasp or scraper, or with coarse sandpaper wrapped around a piece of doweling.

The bottom of a casting may be hollowed out shortly after it is poured if it is a slow-setting material. Scoop or press out a channel when it has thickened to a puttylike consistency.

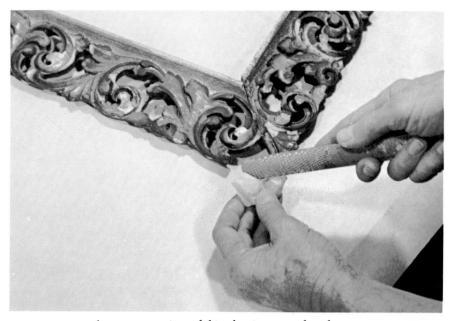

A convex rasp is useful in shaping curved surfaces.

3. Use a file, sandpaper, and fine-toothed saw to trim and shape the casting until it fits. Glue it in place and blend it into surrounding ornamentation with plastic wood.

4. Smooth the surface very lightly with 8/0 finishing paper, and give the new ornament several coats of gesso.

Final shaping and fitting of new ornament is done with a small saw, file, and sandpaper.

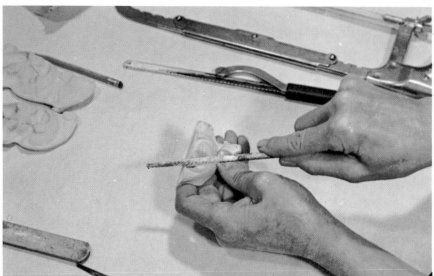

9

Ready-made Ornaments

OCCASIONALLY WE SEE A FINE ANTIQUE THAT HAS LOST AN IMPORTANT ORNAMENT and has no facsimile from which to cast a duplicate. The ornament may have been a carved basket of flowers, a griffin, the head of a Grecian goddess, or an embossed border. Perhaps we can only guess at what ornament filled the vacant space.

This calls for some inventiveness. If you can carve or model in wood or clay, you may create a replacement that harmonizes with the general style of the antique. If you are not so talented, you must either enlist the services of an artist or obtain a ready-made ornament.

Fortunately, all sizes, shapes, and period styles of architectural ornaments and borders are available from commercial suppliers. They are made of plaster, wood fiber, or other composition materials; some are carved from real wood. Illustrations of ready-made ornaments and borders are shown on pages 81 and 82.

Examples of ready-made ornaments and borders. Hundreds of designs are available from manufacturers. They may be glued in place and painted or gilded like wood. Illustrations shown here and on page 82 were provided by The Decorators Supply Corporation, Chicago.

1/4	3/16	3/8	1/8
3/8	1/4	5/8	3/16
5/8	5/16	3/8	1/8
5/8	1/4	5/8	3/16
1/4	3/16	1/4	1/8
3/8	3/16	3/8	1/8
1/4	3/16	3/4	3/16
5/16	3/16	1/2	1/8
3/8	1/4	5/8	3/16
5/8	3/8	7/8	1/4
3/8	3/16	1 1/8	3/16
3/8	1/8	3/8	1/8
5/8	3/16	5/8	3/16
7/8	1/4		

10

Things Gold Leaf
Can Beautify

GOLD LEAF CAN DECORATE SO MANY KINDS OF THINGS THAT THE QUESTION OFTEN is not *can* it, but *should* it be used. Gold leaf on large objects bespeaks formality. Informal "country" furnishings were not meant to be gilded, excepting a few objects such as picture and mirror frames, on which the gilding was usually quite restrained. If you cover a country piece with gold leaf it looks absurdly unconvincing, and may leave the impression that you are trying to make a silk purse out of a sow's ear—even though the country piece is a fine antique. It is of course accepted that ornately carved and gilded objects are out of place in a decor of plain, informal simplicity. It is also accepted that tastefully inspired arrangement can make some curious combinations blend beautifully.

Today many small, new objects are sold unfinished, to be decorated by hobbyists in decoupage, ceramics, and other arts and crafts. Many of these objects lend themselves to gold leafing. As examples, we describe the treatment of three small wooden boxes, made for decoupage, and two pieces of bisque from ceramics molds. These new items, unfinished, cost only a few dollars each. The carved eagle console table discussed on a following page was made about 1730 and is valued at more than four thousand dollars. The range in type and value of things that gold leaf can beautify is unlimited.

On the following pages are illustrations of how gold leaf, silver leaf, composition leaf, and bronzing powders may be used to gild various objects. Detailed instructions for all procedures are contained on preceding pages.

Three Wooden Boxes

Each of the three new boxes shown on this page is being gilded with a different material. All three will receive the same preparatory treatment. It is: (1) six coats of gesso; (2) smoothing, first with 6/0 finishing paper, then with 4/0 steel wool; (3) two coats of thinned orange shellac; and (4) final smoothing with 4/0 steel wool. Then each box is given a different kind of gilding.

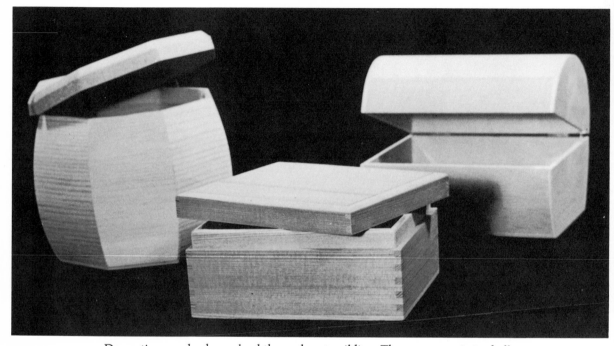

Decorative wooden boxes lend themselves to gilding. They are an artistic challenge to devotees of decoupage.

Foundation coatings of gesso are applied to seal the bare wood and make a smooth cushion for gilding. The first coat is thinned to insure penetration of the open grain.

Gessoed surfaces are smoothed evenly with finishing paper wrapped around a wooden block. Final smoothing with steel wool follows.

An Octagon Box

The octagon box is being coated with genuine gold and silver leaf—gold on the top and silver on the sides. When all leaf has been applied, the box is put aside overnight to allow the oil-type size to harden. Then it is rubbed lightly but briskly with absorbent cotton to remove loose edges of overlapping leaf. A ready-made ornament, leafed with silver, is fastened in place with epoxy glue on the gold-leafed top. Finally, the box is given two coats of thinned, clear shellac to prevent the silver leaf from tarnishing.

Silver leaf is applied over oil-type size with a gilder's tip. If handled carefully, silver leaf may be picked up and laid in place with the fingers.

Only a good grade of absorbent cotton is used to rub off overlapping edges of leaf. Inferior grades contain impurities that may scratch the surface.

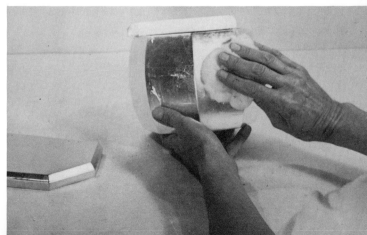

The ready-made ornament being glued in place was ordered from a manufacturer's catalog. It has been silver leafed, for contrast with the gold-leafed top.

An Oblong Box

The oblong box is being gilded with an antique-gold shade of metallic bronzing powder; the powder contains no real gold. First, the box is coated with oil-type size. When the size reaches the right tackiness, the powder is dusted over it. The box is allowed to stand overnight, the excess powder is blown off, and the surface is gently wiped with a soft cloth. It is then given two light coats of clear, acrylic spray before being handled. Ready-made ornaments are enameled white and glued in place.

A 1-inch camel hair dusting brush is used to dust bronzing powder over the sized surface. Excess powder is poured back into the container.

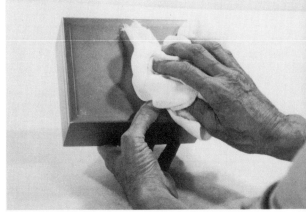

It is important to wipe all loose bronzing powder from the surface before handling the box. If this is not done, fingerprints may result.

An acrylic spray prevents tarnishing. The spray is started with the nozzle pointed away from the box, so the first unvaporized drops will not cause spots.

A Trunk-shaped Box

The trunk-shaped box is being gilded with composition (imitation) gold leaf which, like the bronzing powders, contains no real gold. The leaf is laid with the fingers, over oil-type size. After the box has been leafed, it is put aside for at least 24 hours; when size is covered with the thick, composition leaf, it takes longer to harden.

Overlapping edges of leaf are rubbed off with absorbent cotton, as for the octagonal box. One or two coats of thinned shellac are applied to prevent tarnishing. Finally, an enameled ornament is glued in place.

Oil-type size is applied with a flat, sable brush. The box top is lifted clear of the table, giving the brush access to all parts of the surface.

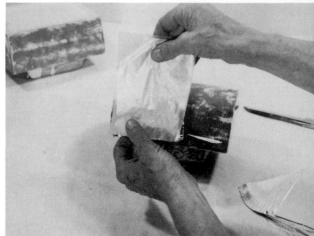

Composition leaf is applied with the fingers. The separating tissue makes it easier to pick up and lay in place without wrinkling.

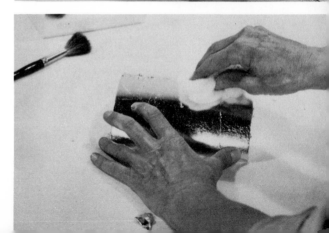

Overlapping edges of composition leaf are thicker and tougher than those of genuine leaf. Brisk rubbing with absorbent cotton removes them.

Gilded boxes can serve many useful and decorative purposes.

Two Pieces of Bisque

The escutcheon and goose shown on this page are small pieces of bisque cast from molds in a ceramics studio. Gilding materials cannot be used satisfactorily to decorate ceramics that have been glazed; the leaf or powder soon scratches or rubs off the hard, vitreous surfaces. Bisque, however, is porous, and takes gilding readily.

A wide variety of decorative bisque figures are sold at small cost by ceramics shops.

The Escutcheon

Red enamel, and silver and gold bronzing powder, will decorate this escutcheon. The enamel is applied first, to the entire piece, since the porous surface must be sealed.

After the enamel has dried, parts of the design to be silvered are coated with oil-type size; a tiny (No. 0) flat sable brush is used. When the size is tacky, silver powder is dusted over it, and the size is allowed to harden overnight.

The piece is then sprayed with a clear acrylic coating, and the parts to receive gold powder are given the same treatment, with a final coating of spray.

Gold bronzing powder is dusted over the tacky size with a camel hair dusting brush, as was done for the oblong box.

The fresh enamel is allowed to stand for 3 or 4 days. If it is not thoroughly dry, the bronzing powders will adhere to the wrong places.

The Goose

Genuine gold leaf will be used for the goose. It will be applied over yellow burnish size. If the bisque surface is smooth, gesso is not needed. Six coats of yellow burnish size are applied and the surface is smoothed with 4/0 steel wool—*not with finishing paper.* Then the leaf is laid, and is burnished with an agate burnisher.

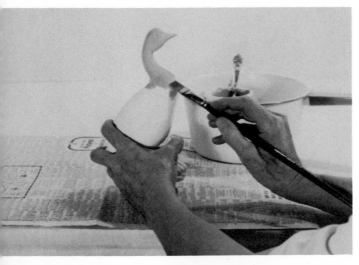

Either yellow or red burnish size may be used. Usually, yellow is preferred for an object subject to handling.

Loose-packed gold leaf is applied with a gilder's tip.

After the leaf is laid, gilding is completed by burnishing the object with an agate burnisher.

A golden goose contemplates a gilded escutcheon.

A Rare Antique Table

The hand-carved console table shown here has been put in sound physical condition. It has received a gesso foundation. Restoration will be completed with both mat and burnished gold leaf, and enamel.

After more than two centuries of use and wear, this antique table has earned the restoration it now is receiving. Here, the base coatings of gesso have been applied.

The procedure, step by step, is:

1. Two coats of *yellow* burnish size are applied to the entire table, except sides of the base and the rocks on which the eagle stands. Three more coats of *red* burnish size are applied to the eagle's beak, eye, and talons, and to the high tips of the feathers. Beak, eye, and talons are smoothed with 4/0 steel wool.

(The yellow size serves to cover hard-to-reach hollows and crevices with a goldlike color, and to mark the areas that will be mat leafed.)

2. Gold leaf to be burnished is laid over areas covered with red size. Then the beak, eye, and talons are given a high burnish; the high surfaces of the feathers are burnished lightly.

Burnish size covers all areas except those that will be enameled.

Leaf is laid on burnish size. Carved areas require more leaf than smooth, flat surfaces.

Burnishing the carved feathers requires patience, but the results are rewarding.

3. The yellow size covering low parts of the feathers is sealed with shellac. Yellow size on the apron (at top) and the carved border on the base is first smoothed with steel wool, then shellacked.

4. All yellow areas are mat leafed over oil-type size; loose-packed leaf is used on the feathers, and patent leaf on the carved borders and the waves of the apron frieze.

Patent leaf is easily pressed onto raised waves of the apron, over oil-type size.

A stiff, bristle brush is used to press patent leaf into carved hollows of the border. Many gilders prefer to use loose-packed leaf, applied with a gilder's tip.

Additional pieces of *loose* leaf are laid on the border and brushed into the deep carving to reach uncovered spots.

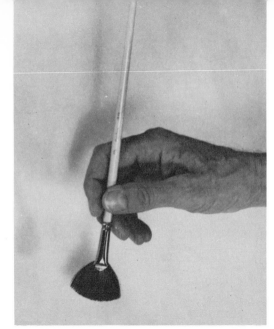

A delicate brush, called a *fan blender*, is nicely suited for dusting particles of gold leaf into deep places.

5. Liquid gilt is used to touch out small bare spots in hollows, where the leaf did not reach.

6. The carved rocks on which the eagle stands are enameled dull black; the apron rail is enameled an antique green.

Flat black enamel on the carved rocks makes the burnished talons stand out in high contrast. The severe dullness of the black is relieved by a final coating of eggshell (very dull) varnish.

Dull, green enamel harmonizes with the gold. Some paint manufacturers have reproduced color shades that were popular in the eighteenth century.

7. The final step is to faintly darken gilded recesses and hollows with brown varnish stain dulled with a little rottenstone.

The finished table is a thing of gilded beauty that can be a joy, not forever, but possibly for a few more centuries.

Other Objects

The following illustrations show how gold leaf can beautify a wide variety of things and lift them from mediocrity to elegance. These objects were gilded by the procedures described on the foregoing pages of this book.

Gold leaf and enamel replace the original stained-wood finish of this clock.

A ready-made ornament, in sections, is placed for gluing.

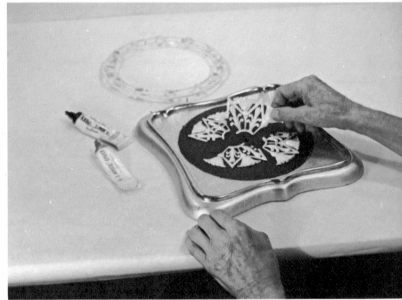

A Chinese bamboo tray on spider legs is decorated with enamel and gold leaf.

There is no real gold on this delicate chair. It has been gilded with bronzing powder over oil-type size.

Real gold and agate burnishing have made
these plaster figurines live again.

The case of this old German clock is made
of walnut. The original finish was stain
and varnish; no gold.

99

The composition (imitation) gold leaf on this table has been coated with white shellac to prevent tarnishing.

Old pieces of furniture can be beautified by restoring their gold trim.

11

Care of Brushes

MOST BRUSHES USED IN GILDING ARE EXPENSIVE. YOU CAN PROLONG THEIR LIVES—
and turn out better work—if you clean them thoroughly after each using. Do
it immediately, or the material you have applied will harden in the hairs.

After using a brush, clean it in three or four rinses of the material's base
solvent. That is, if you applied varnish or paint that had a turpentine base,
use turpentine (or mineral spirits) to clean the brush. For shellac, use alcohol;
for lacquer, use lacquer thinner; for water-base paints, use soap and water.
Brushes used for oil-type gold sizes are cleaned in turpentine; those used for
gesso and burnish size are cleaned in water. Container labels usually name
the base solvent in which brushes should be cleaned.

When the brush is thoroughly clean, press it dry with a cloth or newspaper. If you have rinsed it in turpentine or mineral spirits, give it a final
washing with soap and warm water.

Brushes that are used daily need be cleaned only once or twice a week if
you keep the hairs immersed in the proper cleaning solvent. There are
convenient brush holders for this purpose. Use a separate brush holder for
each type of solvent.

Illustrations of brushes used in gilding are shown on the following pages.

A convenient holder, for keeping brushes in good condition while in use.

a. Flat sable. The most useful of all gilding brushes.

b. Large round sable. For wetting burnish size.

c. Small round sable. For spotting and antiquing.

d. Camel hair quill. For touching leaf into place.

e. Camel hair wash brush. Used as duster.

f. Stencil brush. For cleaning carved hollows.

g. Flat bristle. For thick coatings.

h. Gilder's tip.

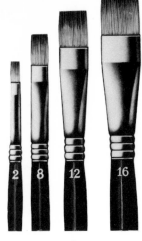

a.

Brushes used in gilding, shown about two-thirds actual size; the gilder's tip is about one-third actual size. Brushes are a gilder's best friend—when they are of good quality and when the right brush is used for each purpose. Illustrations shown here are by courtesy of M. Grumbacher, Inc., New York.

12

Gilding Supplies

IF YOU LIVE IN A LARGE CITY, ALL THE SUPPLIES YOU NEED WILL BE AVAILABLE IN retail stores. First, contact the art-supplies stores. Materials they do not handle are sold by paint, hardware, ceramics, and art-crafts stores. The telephone book and yellow pages can save a lot of legwork.

In small cities and rural areas you may be unable to get even such basic requirements as gold leaf and sable brushes. Then you have a choice of two things—either persuade local retailers to stock the items you need, or order them by mail from manufacturers who will serve the retail trade. The first course is by far the better: you can more conveniently buy the materials locally as you need them; and by stocking them, your retailer will build sales of new items to other customers.

If you must order by mail, the following list of suppliers will serve as a guide. In establishing your contacts, we suggest that you ask the suppliers to send you information about their retail quantities and prices.

Some Suppliers of Gilding Materials

Abrasive papers (sandpaper, finishing paper.) Paint stores; hardware stores.

Agate burnishers. H. Behlen & Bro., Inc., 10 Christopher St., New York, N.Y. 10014. Write for description and prices.

Alcohol, denatured. Paint stores; hardware stores.

Alginate impression powder. Dental supply firms. Or ask your dentist to order for you.

Aluminum leaf. See *Gold leaf.*

Base plate wax. Dental supply firms. Or ask your dentist to order for you.

Borders, carved. See *Ornaments, ready-made.*

Bronzing powders. Art-supplies stores; paint stores.

Brushes. Art-supplies stores. (A leading manufacturer is M. Grumbacher, Inc., 460 West 34th St., New York, N.Y. 10001. This company does not sell to the consumer, but will fill orders from your local retailer.)

Burnishers, agate. See *Agate burnishers.*

Burnish size. See *Sizes.*

Casting materials. Ceramics studios; art-crafts shops. For mold rubber, fiber filler, separating liquids, and casting plasters, write to Permanent Pigments, Inc., Cincinnati, Ohio 45212.

Colorants, varnish. Paint stores. Tinting colorants trade-named Tints-All are manufactured by Sheffield Bronze Paint Corp., 17814 Waterloo Rd., Cleveland, Ohio 44119.

Composition gold leaf. See *Gold leaf.*

Copper leaf. See *Gold leaf.*

Distilled water. Drugstores; grocery stores.

Doweling. Hardware stores; lumberyards.

Dry colors. Art-supplies stores.

Epoxy glue, "5-minute." Paint stores; hardware and hobby shops. Manufactured by Devcon Corp., Danvers, Mass. 01923.

Gesso, dry mixture. Art-supplies stores. Or write to Permanent Pigments, Inc., Cincinnati, Ohio 45212.

Gold leaf. Hastings & Co., Inc., Gold Leaf Division; Dutton & Darnell Rds., Philadelphia, Pa. 19154. Also manufactures silver, aluminum, and composition leaf.

Liquid gilt. Art-supplies stores.

Moldings. See *Ornaments, ready-made.*

Mold rubber. See *Casting materials.*

Oil-type sizes. See *Sizes.*

Ornaments, ready-made. The Decorative Supply Corp., 3610 South Morgan St., Chicago, Ill. 60609. Manufactures ornaments, moldings, and decorative borders in wood fiber, composition, and plaster. Write for information about illustrated catalogs.

Paint remover. Paint stores; hardware stores.

Paints, antique colors. Turco Paint and Varnish Co., 212 Race St., Philadelphia, Pa. 19106.

Plastic wood. Paint stores; hardware stores.

Rottenstone. Paint stores; hardware stores.

Sandpaper. See *Abrasive papers.*

Shellac. Paint stores.

Sizes. Hastings & Co., Inc., Gold Leaf Division; Dutton & Darnell Rds., Philadelphia, Pa. 19154. Manufactures all sizes used in gilding.

Spray, clear acrylic. Art-supplies stores.

Steel wool. Paint stores; hardware stores.

Turpentine. Paint stores.

Varnish, varnish stain. Paint stores.